DENNIS FLANDERS'
BRITANNIA

To Mr. Irving Goldstein.

Dennis Flanders.

IGHTHAM MOTE, 1934

DENNIS FLANDERS'
BRITANNIA

BEING A SELECTION FROM THE WORK

of

DENNIS FLANDERS

R.W.S.   R.B.A.

WHO FOR HALF A CENTURY

HAS

OBSERVED, DRAWN & LOVED

THE

LANDSCAPE & ARCHITECTURE

of the

BRITISH ISLES

ORIEL PRESS
STOCKSFIELD

BOSTON   HENLEY   LONDON

MELBOURNE

Dennis Flanders' Britannia
© *1984, Dennis Flanders*

First published in 1984 by Oriel Press Limited
Stocksfield, Northumberland, England, NE43 7NA.
3 Chesterfield Hill, Mayfair, London, W1X 7RG.
9 Park Street, Boston, Mass. 02108, U.S.A. and
6th Floor, 464 St. Kilda Road, Melbourne,
Victoria 3004, Australia.

Set in Baskerville and printed by
Knight & Forster, Leeds.
Colour separations by Spectrum Photolitho, Bradford.

Trade enquiries to
Routledge & Kegan Paul PLC
Broadway House, Newtown Road, Henley-on-Thames, Oxon, R99 1EN.

ISBN 0 85362 206 X

THE TITLE OF THIS BOOK ACKNOWLEDGES
THAT OF WILLIAM CAMDEN
WHOSE BRITANNIA WAS
PUBLISHED FOUR
CENTURIES
AGO

TO DALMA

ACKNOWLEDGEMENTS

A number of pictures in this book could not have been included but for the kindness of various people and institutions who have extended their ownership of the copyright. Chief among these are the Proprietors of *The Illustrated London News*, (Pages 26, 42, 47, 58, 78, 91, 93, 115, 142, 162, 166, 173, 197, 206, 211, 219, 222, 223), and of *The Sunday Times* (Pages 90, 143, 170, 171, 174, 186, 206), and to these great newspapers the publisher and I extend our hearty thanks.

There are publishers, too, that I wish to thank: in particular John Sands Ltd. of Sydney (one of the oldest printing firms in Australia) for their beautiful reproductions of two of the London drawings (Pages 212, 213), and Delgado Ltd., formerly of London now of Burnley, for the picture on Page 204.

It is by courtesy of the Trustees of the Imperial War Museum that we have been able to include the drawing of the bomb-damage at St. Stephen's Walbrook in London (Page 214) and the Guildhall Library, City of London, for the picture entitled *The Towers of Westminster* (Page 215).

There are others also, whom we wish to thank: The Governor and Company of the Bank of England for giving me access to their premises near St Paul's, from which the drawing on Page 218 was made, and for acquiring the original (could one receive a nicer compliment?). Others who have shown similar kindness are: the Deans and Chapters of Westminster Abbey, St George's Chapel, Windsor, Christ Church Cathedral, Oxford and the Commandant of the Police College, Bramshill House, Hampshire.

The artist, in particular, wishes to thank Clients and Galleries who have commissioned works or bought them at exhibitions, and to express a debt of gratitude for such appreciation, which does, indeed, keep my family and myself alive! In this connection I would mention Sir Philip Goodhart, MP, for he has, as far as I am aware, the largest collection of my works outside the Guildhall Library.

The following too, have helped in the preparation of this book: The Rev. Peter Mold, now vicar of a Parish in Western Australia, formerly a curate in Boston, Lincolnshire, for sending back a picture, who, whilst a theological student in Lincoln, kept me going with glasses of sherry when I was making a drawing of that glorious Cathedral from his window; Mrs. Julyan Mulock of Ontario for also sending back a drawing across the sea for reproduction; Mr David Alexander and Mr James Stirk for allowing me the use of their own houses situated in areas difficult of quick or easy access.

Next on my list of acknowledgements is the firm of A. C. Cooper Ltd, who have photographed the bulk of the works in this book. Their photographic excellence has been consistently high and I willingly sing their praises; our association has lasted since 1942.

These notes would not be complete without mentioning my indebtedness to my wife and family for their continued help and encouragement over many years — for they have shared in all the pleasures, pains, frustrations and triumphs; and finally my heartfelt thanks to Mr Bruce Allsopp, my publisher and his colleagues, for it would be impossible to imagine a more enthusiastic and resourceful partner for such a project, and without whom this book might never have seen the light of day.

DENNIS FLANDERS
LONDON 1984

CONTENTS

LIST OF PLATES

SIZE OF PICTURES

Most of the pictures in this book are reproduced from originals which measure about 18 inches by 14 inches.

x

INTRODUCTION

THE CONCEPTION of this book actually took place as long ago as 1936 and I can remember the exact hour and place. It was in Oxford Street, London, on the pavement outside Selfridge's, at about 1 pm, during the lunch hour, near my place of work. I was looking into the window of Bumpus' bookshop (it has now gone) and what I saw there has determined the course of my life ever since.

Let me explain. I was twenty-one at the time, and although in 'gainful occupation' (at £1 a week!) was not at all satisfied with my job in a firm of fashionable interior decorators, interesting as it was. Certainly my bent was artistic; there could be no doubt about that, as I had never ceased to draw and sketch since the age of five, and this job did indeed include a certain amount of drawing; but it was not leading in the direction in which I wished to go. Not that I had any clear idea of what direction that should be. What sort of drawing? and how could I earn a living that way? They were very important questions, for drawing was the only thing I was any good at. At that time therefore, what I awaited was a hint or sign to help me. I had already been attending evening classes at the Regent Street Polytechnic in antique drawing and the life class. My mother, who was a painter and miniaturist, encouraged me to do this, and had, indeed, paid the modest fee for evening students, twenty-five shillings a year, I believe.

Incredibly boring though this was I had an instinctive feeling that such work was marvellous training for *seeing* things correctly — so I stuck at it. But what particularly appealed to me were *pictures* of towns and villages, buildings of great beauty and interest, cathedrals and castles and the like, and I had been through a period of considering taking up architecture as a career. A part of the studies at the Polytechnic had been in the field of interior decoration and some of this had been historical studies. They took the form of making measured-drawings of doorways, mantelpieces, ironwork, lectures on heraldry in the Victoria and Albert Museum and, in the summer, outdoor sketching in the Parks and the Temple. It was all absolutely fascinating. Thus, I became ready to undertake some form of creative work.

The early twenties, (I refer to years of age) are the time of burgeoning activity. Keenness and power are unleashed and lucky indeed are those who recognise a task that can be done. This was the condition I found myself in on that day. What I was gazing at, in this bookshop-window, was about a dozen magnificent drawings (or rather reproductions of drawings) the like of which I had never seen before. They were by Muirhead Bone and their subject matter was Spain; its towns, cathedrals, its palaces, ports and its people. They were pages of a book shortly to be published in a very large format, only two hundred and fifty copies to be printed at one hundred guineas. The splendour of these drawings and their subject matter were something quite beyond my experience at that time. The detail, the animation of figures and animals, the restrained colour and, above all, the spirit of calm dignity that seemed to breathe from every drawing was a revelation to me, as was the astonishing effect that could be realised by using charcoal and pencil, with pen and ink and water-colour. At last, I saw what could be done (for I sensed that this was the type of subject that appealed to me more than any other) — and so, in a flash . . . 'You can keep all your Madonnas and Saints, Gods and Goddesses, dark portraits of dead Kings and compositions of shot pheasants and deer. You can also keep your badly drawn "impressions" and the like.' (I have since revised my ideas somewhat') 'This is the stuff for me' said I to myself — but why Spain? What about England? And then I knew. It would be I that would do it. So then and there I made up my mind to do the same for England (or rather Britain, as it turned out). And this, in one way or another, is what I have been doing ever since.

Walmer Castle

xi

But how to begin, and earn a living at the same time? That was the burning question. It is a curious thing that when you want particularly to achieve something the opportunity to do so seems to present itself, sooner or later. If you are single-minded enough you find a way to do it. I suppose the mind dwells upon the problem incessantly and eventually solves it. In this case it was obvious that I had to continue in my job (it was with Maurice Adams, Interior Decorator, the son of the more famous Maurice Adams, the architect of Bedford Park) but try, in what little spare time there was, to make drawings (as *pictures*, I mean) and sell them.

But I lacked experience and so needed to change my job — if possible to work for a printer in some way, so as to understand methods of printing. I was helped to this conclusion by being on friendly terms with the artist, Hanslip Fletcher, to whom I had been introduced while still at school when he had come to give a lecture on his work. This had been very stimulating, and as it was given during the lunch-hour on one of the days when I was taking the School Certificate Examination, it enabled me to pass, cheered on by the idea that life could be so enthralling.

In his time (between the Wars and after the Second) he was a man extremely well-known, by his lively pen and ink drawings of street scenes and beauty-spots of London, and other places, that appeared week-by-week, in the pages of the *Sunday Times*. Frequently I saw him in the streets, his stool placed on a collapsible card-table, (for he preferred to work standing up, scribbling away at some jolly scene, or concentrating studiously, and we would have a chat. As our friendship grew, he invited me to come sketching with him and I began to see how I could earn a living. The idea came dimly at first but as desire grew, I saw clearly what had to be done. Quite simply, the same thing! But with another newspaper or magazine.

As for the extra experience I needed, I began looking at the advertisement columns of the *Daily Telegraph* to find a job that would teach me *what* I needed to know, and quite soon, such a notice appeared. This is how it ran. 'Young artist required to copy photographs of houses, pets etc., onto zinc plate with 4H pencil, so that results will look like original drawings, Salary £2.10.0'. I applied for the job and got it. It was September at the time and I worked at these drawings until

Christmas, when such work came to an end, of course, and then, in January, I was instructed to make ruled-lines for the pages of ledgers. I mentally rebelled and wanted to leave and set myself up as a free-lance artist. Telling this to my mentor (for such Hanslip had now become) he said 'not yet, it is still cold. Hold on until April and *then* try if you must'. How wise he was! So I carried on for a little and then began making ghastly mistakes and duly got the sack. You see, I was terrified of handing in my notice, as my Father would have been furious and disappointed. He was a musician, and the time was still the hungry thirties, you must remember. We had very little money then.

So, in that very April, I had taken the irretrievable step of setting up as a free-lance artist. It was 1937, and during that first week, there was printed in the local press *The Walthamstow Guardian* the news that our Bishop, the Bishop of Barking was retiring and leaving his home, a rather lovely old early nineteenth century building, and leaving the district. I rushed there, called, asked his permission to draw it, did so, took the pen and ink result down to the local paper; it was published (fee 10/6d); the Bishop bought the original, other members of the family ordered replicas, and at the end of a fortnight, I had earned three times what I would have done had I remained in that prosaic printing works in the Farringdon Road, London.

This went on for quite a time, only using pen and ink which is a difficult medium but capable of great boldness, charm and finesse. It gives a silvery look and goes beautifully with printed matter. It is an ideal way of decorating a book, magazine or paper, when only black and white is required. It is also the cheapest method of reproduction.

Hatfield House

Then one day I took a drawing of the famous Trafalgar Tavern at Greenwich to 'Peterborough's' office of the *Daily Telegraph* and met the famous Hugo Wortham, who apart from publishing the drawing, became a firm friend and exerted enormous influence on me. He was an admirer of everything excellent in all the arts — and in people too. Sometimes he would ring me up and ask me to draw something for his column. It was always very worthwhile and some of the paragraphs he wrote to go with the sketch were masterpieces of their kind.

One thing I would like to write here, by way of advice to a young artist, is this. Always try and get your picture back after publication. You can then sell it, and thus have two sources of income. Publishers and Editors have a habit of wrapping you artwork in brown paper parcels and hiding them for years — in fact until after your death and then bringing them out and having a sale, which will not benefit you! Hugo Wortham gave me back mine and there was never any question of not doing so. But he was the exception, rather than the rule.

And so life went on, with modest success. Every now and then, I went off to make drawings and water-colours of my own choosing, when I had collected a little extra money, very economically staying at Youth Hostels, often with a particular friend, George Whitby, who became a brilliant architect and partner of Donald MacMorran R.A., but died very suddenly a few years ago. (He designed the new extension to the Old Bailey). Our particular favourite spots to walk over and sketch were the Sussex Downs and the Cotswold Hills. They became very familiar to us.

Funeral Barge of Sir Winston Churchill 1965

Then the War came, and for a time I joined the St. Paul's Watch, and went through all the period of the bombing of London. It would be a wicked lie to say I enjoyed it (in retrospect it seems, of course, almost unbelievable and certainly obscene) but the exciting visual effects of ruined streets, gutted churches, floors strewn with charred timbers, tottering walls, with streaks of purple and crimson caused by heat, melted lead with silver streaks, huge holes in the ground, all these had a profound effect on my work in three ways.

Firstly I was impelled to draw as many of the beautiful buildings that still stood, before they might be destroyed; secondly, to make pictures of the ruins (for so many of them were impressive beyond belief) and thirdly, the deep effect it had on my technique. The black pen and ink was totally inadequate, useless to portray the subject matter created by the effects of the bombing raids. This was the time when I summoned to my aid, charcoal, carbon-pencil, water-colour, chalk, brown ink (instead of black) and a number of other media — tinted paper, for instance. All this took charge and released me from the thraldom of *only* pen and ink (although I have never really given it up and still occasionally send in a 'pen and ink' to the *Daily Telegraph*), and led me to make 'free-er' drawings that were, at the same time, pictures rather than mere sketches. I then paid short visits to other cities that had been desecrated: Bristol, Bath, Exeter, Canterbury and York, and found marvellous subjects to draw. Many of the works produced then are now in the Imperial War Museum, while those of London are in the Guildhall Collection.

With regard to the St. Paul's Watch, I want to pay tribute to Godfrey Allen, the Surveyor to the Fabric, who organised the 'Watch'. It is through him and him alone that St. Paul's was not destroyed. A large patrol was on duty every night and although the fabric had two direct high explosive hits, no fires were started, all being put out by water and sometimes even kneeling hassocks. I always maintain that if all buildings had been guarded by enough watchers, many more buildings would have been saved. The worst raids were always at week-ends, when most Londoners, even those on fire-watch duties, went away for the week-end. I often feel that if we had lost the war, it would have been because of our 'week-end' habit.

Then in 1942, I joined the Army, going first of all to a depot outside Cardiff, which, contrary to my previous ideas, I found a most beautiful city, surrounded by glorious country, rivers, mountains and valleys. After various postings, I joined the Royal Engineers at the School of Military Engineering at Ripon in Yorkshire, to which it had been moved from its home base at Chatham. Here, still with my drawing and painting tackle, I found myself in company with other artists, who all, since those days, have achieved high renown. There was Terence Cuneo (who handles the brush with tremendous verve), Ernest Greenwood, who is now President of the Royal Society of Water-Colour Painters, Claude Page, a fine black and white artist and James Porteous Wood, one of the great designers of Asprey's for many years, but also a fine painter of the Scottish mountains on whose shoulders the mantle of D.Y. Cameron has fallen. We became particular friends at Ripon and together, on bicycles, we explored the Dales and plains of Yorkshire, myself being influenced by his painting and he by my drawing. A mutual admiration society is always a good thing. The considerable time I remained at Ripon was productive of many drawings (including a dozen or so in this book) and gave me an abiding love of the North.

I must mention one unpleasant experience I went through. As there were so many artists in the Forces there, we held one or two Exhibitions in the Town Hall, one in aid of 'Help the Russians Fund' and another for the Chinese. I, as one of the organisers was deeply involved and had indeed asked everybody to the opening, including the Commandant, the Mayor, the Dean, the Bishop, and Lady Swinton who had agreed to open the first Exhibition. One night, I awoke suddenly and wondered whether the floor might give way under the weight of all the local dignitaries — How terrible! I thought, but it was twelve hours before I could call upon the City Engineer to ask him about it. I did so and he said 'Pooh, it will be alright if they don't dance!'

I must also express my deep thanks to and appreciation of the immense friendliness shown to us by the people whose native county it was, and into whose midst we had been thrust. So many people of all kinds opened their houses to us and indeed many marriages took place... But this was, of course, the common lot in all parts of Britain during those years. For us, we gained the friendship of many which still endures.

Back in civilian life, in 1946, I returned to the pen and ink/newspaper syndrome, and was lucky enough to be asked to make drawings for the *Yorkshire Post*. I had met the Editor, Sir Linton Andrews, before and showed him my work, but there was a delay due to the shortage of newsprint for a year or two. He then asked me to make a series of drawings of various beauty-spots and afterwards of 'Yorkshire Industries' which included woolsheds, shipbuilding yards, ironworks, steelworks, etc.

This lasted a year or so, and then quite suddenly, when I took in a drawing he said 'I can get a photograph of this. I don't want a drawing of something that can be photographed'. Dumbfounded, I simply refused to do any more. If he thought a drawing was a mere substitute for a photograph, and did not appreciate it for its own sake, I would certainly not try to inflict any more on him! And then came the work for the *Birmingham Post* followed by the *Sunday Times*. But the subject is becoming boring and I must go and write of other things. As for instance getting married!

It was in 1952 that Dalma and I married. We had known each other for a long time, and I should have asked her earlier — but there it is, and we've lived happily ever since.

In 1956, my ambition to draw for the *Illustrated London News* officially (who had actually accepted a number of submissions for several years) was realised, when that renowned Editor, Sir Bruce Ingram asked me to be one of "our special artists", thereby joining the ranks of all those famous names since the journal was founded in 1842.

Many fascinating and wonderful subjects were attempted — and some of the work reproduced in colour. After a long time, our great Editor, who had encouraged me so much (he was a great collector, particularly of sea-pieces) died and his chair was occupied by his nephew, Hugh Ingram, who had been groomed for the job.

In the meantime however, Lord Thomson had acquired the *Illustrated London News* and added it to his collection of newspapers. He let it run on as usual until after Sir Bruce's death, and then decided to alter it completely; changed the Editor and most of the contributors, including me. (Many of these drawings appear in this book).

So, in 1964, it was a case of "all change" and

knowing full well that there was no other journal in all the world that would or could print drawings as big or as well, I decided to draw and paint what I wished, for my own pleasure: and cut myself off from artistic journalism. And so the matter stands today. Exhibiting here and there in certain commercial galleries, having one-man shows, agents, friends, and making especial efforts to be a credit to the Royal Society of Painters in Water-Colours, the Royal Society of British Artists and the Art Workers Guild.

Now to conclude, I would like to write a few words about methods. Without exception, every picture or sketch is done mostly on the spot. Willy nilly one obtains a sense of place and the great "outdoors", and if one stays for a long time, all sorts of delightful effects occur, as shadows move, atmosphere changes, people group themselves — many, many things you see that you would never think of if you were not there. This all adds up the totality of the picture.

I say done mostly on the spot (the conception and all the detail), but this still leaves much to be done afterwards. I find skies and reflections in water are best done away from the scene and in a quiet room where one can lay on big washes in calm and undisturbed comfort, (but one must have already observed what is suitable).

When the subject has been decided upon, I spend much time on choosing the best point of view, which generally means several positions, although none far away from each. For this reason I generally prefer to stand up to draw, in any case to begin with and only sit down on my stool, when I am sure I know what I'm doing.

I justify this idea of moving around, since one walks into a view (or moves from side to side), thus gaining a succession of impressions which add up to the sum of one's delight in the scene, thereby making the picture *more* accurate rather than less.

Now the first sketch is usually done on thin "layout" paper, with an ordinary 2B lead pencil, starting lightly, but getting firmer, generally without rubbing out if possible. Thus, it becomes a cartoon (in the original meaning of the word as a full-sized design for the finished picture). I then trace this on to the sheet of paper to be used for the finished work (usually very smooth and of the finest quality). This tracing is always done very lightly, so that a mere *impression* is indicated, but you have all the main elements of the design in the right place, so can work on the picture with great accuracy of line and tone and without fear of having to rub out!

I like to have a good scheme of light and shade, sunshine and shadow, but the greatest problem for me with the coloured drawings (which is now and has been for many years my main occupation), is *where* to *stop* the line work and take to the brush — in other words, which part of the drawing can best be expressed in line and which in colour. This is, of course, a fascinating problem which changes with every picture.

Brown ink is often used for the line work, in place of pencil. I use carbon pencils a great deal, but I let the subject dictate which medium to use. The ink line gives a bright and better definition, but is apt to jump forward rather in the distances — but I often mix the media, believing that all the different aspects of nature can be rendered best by one particular medium.

But there is another and all-important element that makes a picture come alive, an element without which all the technical knowledge derived from teaching and experience is useless — and that is love; love not only of line and colour but of the subject itself, and it is this that puts poetry into a picture and raises it above the banal.

Readers will find that I have frequently used the word "beautiful" in the captions. Many people today seem chary of using the word, and its opposite "ugly" as if it were merely an expression of opinion and not a fair description. This is because they take too much notice of 'art' experts and critics.

I have no such inhibitions (and I believe that most people agree with me in their inmost hearts). A 'beautiful' landscape, townscape, seascape etc., is one that "delights the eye and hurts not": an ugly one does the opposite, causing depression, sadness and sometimes fury! I think also there is a third word which describes what is banal and causes neither pleasure nor pain but mere indifference. This of course applies to many scenes and places and explains why artists never make pictures of them.

I admit this is a very abstruse subject but it is also of vital importance today when so many are appalled at what they see going up around them. But there is no reason why a new building should be ugly, any more than an old building must be beautiful — we have to *use* our feelings.

Much that is ugly and monstrous and so much

disliked in modern building is because insufficient interest has been taken of aesthetics, i.e., (the look of the thing), practical considerations only being used. In addition, all too little attention is paid to the area or neighbourhood, so that views are obstructed instead of being enhanced: a small handsome, building being overwhelmed by a monstrous one and so on. In my own City of London, I could give examples of insensitive and inappropriate building. Curiously enough it is nearly always a case of architectural bad manners. For example, the Vickers tower fights against the Victoria Tower of the Houses of Parliament: the building at the top of Ludgate Hill arrogantly obscures part of St. Paul's, and a huge, high-rise block jumps up exactly behind the Tower of St. James' Palace which one sees from Piccadilly, as if the designer had never been there to see what would happen.

There is also an inappropriate tower block standing between Waltham Cross and Waltham Abbey on flat land in the middle of the Lea Valley. Another skyscraper (flats I believe) stands up between Lancaster and Morecambe and pulls the eye away from the beautiful hilltop grouping of the church and castle above the river Lune, a composition nearly as good as that of Durham.

But there are recompenses. One can admire the controversial 'Centre Point' — the building that stands at the crossing of Oxford Street and Tottenham Court Road, because it has Form, Scale and Elegance. Housing schemes at both Norwich and York (see p.69) are splendid and appropriate of their kind. I think the reasons are that local traditional building materials have been used and these applied in a human scale. They are a pleasure to look at.

We must also try and alter some of the worst eye-sores left by the Industrial Revolution. I do most of my travelling by train and bus and there are three areas at least that I find ugly, squalid and depressing — the journey between Birmingham and Wolverhampton, from Sheffield to Rotherham (Industrial decline) and from London along the Lea Valley on the line to Cambridge that stretches as far as Enfield Lock. Desperate attempts are being made to plant trees here and there — but it is a long job and one can only hope.

This book then is a paeon of praise for the beauties of these Islands — and a plea to those who, in search of warmth and sunshine abroad unwittingly miss the splendour of their own land, remaining ignorant of what is on their own doorstep, that they should get to know their own inheritance and thereby love and cherish it.

Edinburgh. The Saloon at Messrs Blackwoods, the Publishers
Edinburgh is famous for Doctors and Surgeons, Lawyers, Philosophers and Literary Men. To salute the latter, here is a drawing I was allowed to make of the famous Saloon at Messrs Blackwoods establishment at No. 45 George Street, in the New Town. Here such illustrious writers as Sir Walter Scott, R.L. Stevenson and John Buchan called to discuss their works with the Publishers. This drawing was made just before the building passed to a Building Society in 1972 and the publishing firm retreated to their printing building behind.

SCOTLAND

EDINBURGH, The Lawnmarket
This is part of the Royal Mile that stretches down from the Castle to Holyrood Palace.
Magnificent stone houses, dating from 17th century flank the street on either side, giving
a wonderful idea of the older Scottish townscape. Outside staircases here and there;
crowstepped gables, at the top the odd piece of carved heraldry: all add interest to the
scene, while the centre is dominated by the magnificent Victorian spire of the church of
Tolbooth St. John, darkened by smoke and soot to a glorious black, which my carbon
pencils rendered very well. I am told that services in Gaelic are held here for Highlanders
who come on business to the Capital, for a Capital City Edinburgh certainly is.

EDINBURGH, Holyrood Palace
This is from the lower end of the Royal Mile, here called the Canongate. See how the
"Auld Alliance" has influenced the design of the James IV towers. I very much enjoyed
drawing the texture of the stone on the houses on the left, both excellent examples of the
Scottish love of crowstepped stones as an acceptable design for a gable end.

EDINBURGH FROM CALTON HILL

A source of inspiration to generations of artists. During a visit there some years ago, I climbed up to this beautiful spot each evening (for that seemed the best time) and drew tenderly all the lovely silhouettes. In designing the foreground, I chose several points of view, so as to lead the eye into the various points of interest in the distant city. Each evening seemed more beautiful than the last, and all were different, so I refrained from painting the work until after I returned home — and then, when the various effects seen were sufficiently distilled in my mind, I washed in the colours you see here.

EDINBURGH, "The Heart of Midlothian"
The title of this novel by Sir Walter Scott has always haunted me, and when I came to
know Edinburgh, I sought out a subject for a picture that could bear a similar name. And
here it is; the High Kirk of St. Giles in the centre of the High Street: beyond can be seen
the Tower of the Tron Church and the waters of the Firth of Forth far beyond. The
Mercat Cross, where Proclamations are made; the old Scottish Parliament House and the
Law Courts, are all in close proximity. It is indeed, the Heart of Midlothian, and to prove
it a heart-shaped design is incorporated in the cobble-stones.

ST. ANDREWS, FROM THE LINKS

This reminds one of those early Dutch etchings of mediæval towns, all spires and narrow houses, that could have been sketched by Rembrandt himself. Take a short walk along the beach towards Guard Bridge with the Links on your left (in front, you can see, far away beyond Dundee to the blue Sidlaw Hills), and before you get too far, turn round and you'll see this charming scene. Not many towns in Britain have kept their traditional shape as well as this. With sandwiches and flask, you can spend a very happy day here, watching the tide coming and going. The golf balls fly by over to your right. Nobody worries you; most of those who seem to hang around, are, in fact, hunting for their balls among the long grass — and you may see a seal or two upon the beach.

ANSTRUTHER WESTER, FIFE

Among some very interesting books, inherited from my mother, is a Special Number of
The Studio (1909) called "Sketching Grounds" and in it is a chapter (with illustrations) on
"Coast Towns and Villages of Fife", which interested me enormously. So, when I was in
Edinburgh, I took a long bus ride from Leven to St. Andrews and visited all those
beautiful villages. My family and I subsequently spent several holidays there so that I
have been able to make many drawings of this fascinating area. This particular scene is
very typical.

FALKLAND, WITH FARM BUILDINGS

In Mrs. Oliphant's *Royal Edinburgh* published in 1893 is a wash drawing by George Reid, a Royal Scottish Academician, of Falkland Palace, which seemed to say to me "This is the place for you"! So we went during one of our sojourns in St. Andrews. The charming little town is bursting with subjects to draw, but the particular spot shown on this page (with farm buildings etc.), was difficult to find at first. I feared that the remarkable horse-mill (that eight-sided red tiled building on the right) which showed so prominently in the old drawing, had been demolished.

Using my powers of direction however, and trespassing on private land, a thrill of pleasure struck me as the very view I sought, (sketched by George Reid more than seventy years ago!) burst upon my eyes, looking much finer than I expected. I quickly sized up the situation and was sketching out the composition five minutes later. The hills on the left — the twin Lomonds — I brought inwards a good deal, to give weight to the left boundary of the picture, while some cows, who were wondering who I was, came in usefully to balance the composition on the right. I remember also, that a tree obscured one of the towers of the Palace, Such a pity! So I left it out, to make the picture more readable and easy on the eye.

A very uncomfortable moment came, however, a little later, when the family who owned the farm and the field in which I was sitting arrived in a car, which drew up by the garage doors. A very stern looking lady marched like a grim-faced grenadier over to me and said "May I ask what you are doing on my land?" I am usually afraid of trespassing and rarely do it, so it shows what the power of desire does! I did most earnestly want to find this view having waited years for the chance to do so. I arose from my stool, held out the drawing to her (already half sketched in), doffing my hat, replied 'Madam, I know I have no right to be here, but I have come four hundred miles to make a beautiful picture of your fascinating farm and beautiful town'. Her sternness relaxed, and she said 'I thought you were a Planner and were arranging to demolish us'. Tea was brought out and arrangements were made for another visit on the following day.

The drawing on this page shows the Palace with some of its attendant houses. Also to be seen is the tree that I left out in the picture opposite.

ST MONANCE

This is another irresistible subject to draw. The "Fishermen's Church", small but rugged and dignified, built up out of sloping ground: the interesting memorials and tombstones, each throwing long shadows down the grassy hillside, close cropped by sheep: the foreground bridge over the burn: the row of red-tiled cottages at the end of the town — and, as a background, the blue waters of the Firth of Forth, dotted here and there with a trawler or a yacht; in the far background the grey, pencil line of the Lothian Coast, with the Bass Rock and Salisbury Crags dimly describing their distinctive shapes, makes this a fascinating scene.

CULROSS, page 11

Culross is a place not to be missed. It stands by the Forth upstream from the Bridges. The name is pronouced 'Ku'ross'. On the day early in January that I visited it, the rain did not cease, so I had to find a house with a window giving a suitable view. My second knock produced what I needed. The little window on the ground floor was small, cobwebbed and partially blocked with turnips and kindling, for it was a store, while above resided an elderly lady whom I had seen ascending the outside staircase. She raised no objection and indeed seemed to be charmed with the idea.

For hours I worked, while the rain remorselessly fell and lovely puddles formed in the roadway and the grass verges. At 3 p.m. I had finished, and at the same moment, a door at the top of the staircase opened and my hostess-for-the-day descended with a huge tray laden with buns, bannocks, cream, tea and the like. As payment she explained, (for it was January 4th, and I was her first foot!) I must give her a kiss! I willingly complied with a fat one.

DYSART, page 11

This is the small, rather decayed fishing port of Dysart, standing just east of Kirkaldy. The cliff, topped by trees, marks the end of the domain of *Ravenscraig* now a public park bordering the shore. This drawing was made in late October, when a Londoner might expect the weather here to be somewhat wintry, but sunny day succeeded sunny day, each better than the last, so that I was enjoying St Martin's little summer by the blue waters of the Forth, lapping gently on harbour walls.

11

MELROSE ABBEY, pages 12 and 13
When my wife and I were holidaying in Berwick-upon-Tweed, we took a coach trip which showed us Melrose, Kelso, and Abbotsford, all glorious spots but Melrose took the palm. The beauty of the name, the colour of the stone, the exquisite detail of the windows and its topographical position make Melrose one of the most desirable places I have ever visited in these Islands. The subjects are limitless, quite literally. Two drawings are shown here, but half a dozen would not be enough.

The view on the left with a rainbow (which I had not seen in either a photograph or drawing before) is to my mind one of the most exciting townscapes I have ever seen. But the difficulties of doing it were immense. I *had* to stand in the road — no pavement and no room to sit down, my paint-box poised on a window-sill, traffic continuously coming both ways and hooting me out of the way and the narrowing roadway making a vortex of cold wind. Ugh! But it was done — ultimately. See that marvellous wall on the right. How well it leads the eye towards the Abbey, and what a fine thing it is. I was told Sir Edwin Lutyens designed it, as well he might. His ideas for making Britain beautiful were as good as Wren's — if not better. And the rainbow *did* appear!

The other drawing (above) is much less exciting, but more serene, a feeling I often try to put into a picture. There is a hint too, of some of the exquisite window moulding. There are at least five more marvellous compositions to work out here at Melrose, to which I hope to return.

ABERGELDIE CASTLE, DEESIDE

I was intending to make a water-colour of this scene, but when the pencil work was done, it looked so pleasant that I desisted, and left it as it is. Such a pretty name too!

It was a desire to make a picture of Balmoral Castle that explained my presence in this beautiful area and I found accommodation in a house called "Rhynabaich", above the road and about four miles from the Royal Domain. Occasionally my hostess drove me one way or the other, but on other occasions I walked, passing Abergeldie and sketching it. But in spite of the beauties of the river, the hill and the trees, I was saddened. Every yard or so were the carcasses of wild animals or birds, squashed flat by the tyres of the ubiquitous car. Truly the invention of the internal combustion engine has brought a major tragedy to the world! And — the driver is usually blissfully ignorant of the slaughter he has caused.

MARKINCH

Boldly placed on a knoll right in the centre of this Fifeshire town, St Droston's Church makes an irresistible appeal. The flat tombstones — like dining-room tables — the high banking wall, the turn in the road, the plain stone houses all add up to an interesting picture.

A famous paper-making mill, an equally well-known whisky distillery and a beautiful railway viaduct add lustre to the town.

KELSO ABBEY

Not much of this is left but what does remain is very lovely. One admires the little Square in front of the Gateway and the oblique shadows cast across the stonework by the beech trees. The houses have been trimmed up — an example of the preservation work of the Scottish National Trust.

Kelso itself is full of interest, with an enormous continental style, cobbled Market Place and a splendid bridge like London's own Waterloo Bridge designed by the same Charles Rennie, which Mr. Herbert Morrison, wantonly destroyed in the thirties. Fortunate Kelso!

ST ANDREWS, FROM THE HARBOUR PIER, page 16

This is rather a hackneyed view but certainly none the worse for that. In fact I think it one of the most startling ruins I have ever seen and full of the most romantic historical reminders of some of the terrible happenings that have occurred in this famous University city.

A few fishing boats still sail in and out. There are plenty of glorious red roofs to be seen, and the place is full of very drawable subjects, as is the whole coast of Fife from the Forth Bridges to Dundee. There is also golf!

LINLITHGOW

Half of Linlithgow seems to have been rebuilt lately in the usual drab modern fashion, so strikingly ugly; but much beauty remains. Here in this drawing of the Town Square in the centre of the High Street, is Civic pride and dignity, for Linlithgow is the Capital of the County of West Lothian, sometimes called Linlithgowshire. See the French influence in the ornate Well-head and The Town House with its grand staircase by John Mylne in 1668, the King's Master Mason. Behind is the Church with its new Crown put on in 1965, more than a hundred years after the original one was removed for safety's sake. By its side but not shown in the picture is the Royal Palace. This looks down on a loch and marvellous views of Turneresque quality can be obtained by walking round the water. I look forward to another visit.

ROSLYN CHAPEL, page 19

References to Roslyn Chapel and its unique "apprentice pillar" had long intrigued me, so that when I spent a couple of weeks at Glencorse Barracks at Penicuik two or three years ago, to make some drawings for publication, I took the opportunity of visiting this remarkable building which stands a few miles away

Although services are regularly held here, I found the chapel closed because of vandalism. Since I was unable to enter and also because I arrived on foot from below, as it were (having walked through the beautiful glen from the Barracks) I was rewarded with this striking view which was entirely new to me, and very much more interesting because of that. See how well this unique example of decorated granite looks from below. The guide books write that Rosyln Chapel was founded in 1440 or 1446, by the Earl of Caithness and Prince of Orkney, who intended it to be a great collegiate church but died before even the Choir, which we now behold, was completed.

BALMORAL CASTLE

Distant view from the riverside further up Deeside towards Braemar. The purple hills behind, the blueness of the river, the bright yellow of the gorse bushes, and the dark pinewoods, make this a typical and very beautiful Highland scene.

19

JEDBURGH ABBEY

Jedburgh is the first town you meet in Scotland, if you come from England by the road across Carter Bar. Here you see vast tracts of almost uninhabited country, with frowning Cheviot on your right, and you know for a fact that there *is* a "debatable" land between the two countries, once fought over but now and for so long happily united under the Crown.

The great problem with the composition of this picture, was how so to arrange that the Abbey Tower should stand comfortably near (but not touch) the yew trees on the right hand bank. As you walk round the curve of the road, the whole view discloses itself and you are made to amalgamate several views in one. There was also a rather scruffy spinney on the left, that was not up to standard, so I left it out.

JEDBURGH ABBEY AND THE WATER OF JED, page 20

This is the classic view of Jedburgh Abbey visited by the old romantically minded tourists as well as artists. Both Turner and Girton painted it and it is most instructive to compare the two. Though the surrounding trees have changed, the view is essentially the same, but the amount of water in the Jed, of course changes tremendously, and so do the seasons. This drawing was done in April, during a long series of sunny days but a cold north wind blew incessantly. A thick overcoat and copious flasks of coffee helped to get the task completed.

IRELAND

CORK, SHANDON STEEPLE

When in Cork, I passed this scene on my way down to the river from my Guest House, which stood well up on the western hillside, so I had many opportunities to analyse the scene, as I walked a few hundred yards into it each day. The more I saw of it the more I realised it was a typical urban scene of fifty years ago with absolutely no modern accretions. The rising silhouette of the buildings behind the lower mid-distance was attractive, culminating in the much-loved Shandon Steeple about which many stories and poems abound. The visitor, for a small fee, can climb the tower and play the bells, so that through the day some tune or another is ringing out over the city.

This drawing was done standing up among the crowds of passers by, with my board in the crook of my arm. Many were the conversations I had. The soft low voices of the Irish are a delight to hear and the friendliness is apparent. Freckles abound and there is much sandy hair and when the sun is out, it is a delight to be among the good hearted crowd. I could have kissed them all!

CAHIR CASTLE FROM THE MILL OFFICE

I came to Cahir quite by chance on the way to famous Cashel. Nobody had told me about it, but to find a splendid castle, only partially ruined, set on a huge rock, partly in the middle of a fine river, swollen into a wide mill-pool with a dam nearby and a long mediæval bridge joining the scene together — add to those the Main Street of handsome Georgian houses and shops rising on each bank, with mature and elegant trees, many of them copper beeches — was an unusual experience indeed. Many, many days were spent there, drawing hard, and I have revisited it thrice.

CAHIR, TOWARDS THE CASTLE
This picture shows Cahir Castle standing on its rock in the middle of the River Suir (pronounced "sure"). I was attracted by the contrast of the usual 18th Century town houses and shops with the romantic shape of the splendid castle backed by distant hills, bathed in that wonderful blue one sees only in Ireland. A bright and breezy picture.

CASHEL
A jolly street scene typical of many in Ireland, but with the superb back-cloth of the towers of The Rock of Cashel.

DUBLIN: THE KING'S INNS, page 26
One of the pillars of the Irish legal system, the King's Inns is among the most splendid buildings in the Irish capital. Its name dates back to the assumption by Henry VIII of the title King of Ireland. The present building was begun at the end of the 18th century and finished in the 19th. This was perhaps the golden age of Dublin's architecture and the architect, James Gandon, also built the Four Courts and designed the Custom House which stands so splendidly by the banks of the Liffey. This drawing shows the rather stately "back-door" entrance. The surrounding arch leads through to the park on the other side which is open for public enjoyment.

Dennis Flanders. Cobh

LISMORE CASTLE AND THE RIVER BLACKWATER

This beautiful view was painted on sunny evenings after 5pm in mid-summer during a heat-wave which coincided with my first visit to Ireland. I had seen a photograph of this in an old book and could hardly believe such a view to be true. And it was still just the same. An ideal spot straight out of Arcady!

THE CATHEDRAL AT COBH (pronounced *Cove*), page 28

Although Cork is a port, Cobh, ten miles or so downstream, is called the Port of Cork. This sounds very Irish and of course it is, but Cobh was for the big liners which could not sail up as far as the city itself. Sadly the liners are no more. The great exodus of Irishmen and women usually took place from here and in H.V. Morton's book *In Search of Ireland* can be read a graphic account of the sad partings and farewells that took place a few yards from the scene of this drawing. The dark statue in the centre commemorates another and perhaps even sadder parting. It is reared in memory of those drowned in the monstrous sinking of the *Titanic*, and is by the sculptor Jerome Conor.

The magnificent Cathedral, daringly built on an outcrop of rock, is to the design of E.W. Pugin and G.C. Ashlin, started in 1868 and finished in 1919. Its splendour takes one's breath away.

CORK: South Gate Bridge, St Finbarre's Cathedral and the River Lee.
When I first visited Cork not long ago I wished I had been before, for it seemed there was a lifetime's amount of work to be done. Quite simply, it is beautiful, with all the elements of the finest townscapes imaginable — tidal rivers, bridges, ships, hilly streets, spires, mills, esplanades, parks, beautiful suburbs and the sea not far away.

CORK: St Finbarre's Cathedral from South Gate Bridge, page 30.
This is another version of the same view, but a very different composition. Here, the long wall is the thing, and its very darkness and rough surface make a striking contrast to the smooth white marble of St Finbarre's Cathedral and the joy was to watch the shadow of the central steeple creep slowly over the smaller north-west steeple, and to decide just where the shadow was to be painted. A most beautiful and unexpected subject.

THE QUAY AT WATERFORD

Much had I read about the long quay at Waterford, lined with Georgian façades — the longest quay in Europe, I gather, — more than a mile.

Here it is, with the waters of the River Suir making glorious reflections in the foreground after a boat has gone by. It is a busy port, with much activity going on. The drawing was made from the bridge, which connects the town with the railway station, at which you arrive from Fishguard and Rosslare. The time, just after five o'clock on a sunny evening in June, when the light comes round to the west of the Church towers.

ROCK OF CASHEL

In the golden plain of Tipperary where the milk is creamier and the butter finer, stands the Rock of Cashel once the seat of the Kings of Munster and one of the most hallowed places in Ireland. The town midway upon the road between Dublin and Cork stands at its foot.

Among the buildings crowning the Rock is a cathedral, a church, a round tower of great antiquity, a cross and a hall of choral vicars — all in ruins. It is indeed an astonishing sight. Drawings of close-up scenes were not a success so I ranged the hillsides to the North and East and found this large view. The background hills are those of the Galtee Mountains and the Knockmealdowns, all in that heavenly blue made famous by the paintings of Paul Henry, which reminds me of the following story. An Irish farmer told an American visitor, who complained of how badly the dry stone walls round the fields were built (all full of holes), that the sheep enjoyed looking through the gaps because the lovely blue of the distant mountains made them happy and contented and so yielded more tasty mutton!

The Cathedral was in use in the middle of the 18th century when the Dean, tired of driving up the steep hill each Sunday, closed it in favour of a church down in the town, taking off the roof, in that curious Irish habit, to save rates, or so 'tis said. The old Deanery, a handsome house in the style of Queen Anne is now a hotel which yields a fine view of the Rock from the garden.

WALES

Castle Coch, Glamorganshire.

Denis Flanders
Sep 1942

CASTELL COCH, NEAR CARDIFF

This extraordinary edifice, like a back-cloth for an opera by Wagner designed by King Ludwig II of Bavaria, *was* actually a real castle in ruins when the Victorian Architect William Burgess was asked to restore it, while he was making a superb job of turning Cardiff Castle into a palace.

It stands among trees not far away from Cardiff. You give a gasp of surprise and can scarcely believe your eyes. It is beautifully painted and furnished inside.

LLANGURIG

My excellent friends, the Leopolds of Llanidloes had collected several commissions for me during the winter of 1981/82, so early in the following May, my wife and I found ourselves at this somewhat remote spot near the source of the River Wye. Can one imagine anything more beautiful than this aspect of the village of Llangurig seen across the upper waters of the River Wye?

My desire was to make the main group of trees compose happily with the church tower, which was to be seen at its most attractive angle, while the hill behind was especially fine when the distant tree, towards the right, cut its contour just at the right point.

Although the scene looks tranquil, I kept on moving up and down a hundred yards in order to group the various items into a coherent whole. It took four days working three to five hours each time, while a cold wind from the north west blew constantly.

VALLE CRUCIS ABBEY

This is the loveliest architectural jewel in the far-famed Vale of Llangollen, beloved by so many travellers. You find it a little way off to the right, a mile or two along the Shropshire Union Canal from Llangollen.

As I approached it for the first time, my eyes were assailed by the sight of an enormous collection of caravans, all pale yellow and plastic. Another beauty spot ruined I thought and my heart sank . . . And yet, all was not lost. The caravans were beyond the Abbey so by walking up to them and then turning round, the offensive objects disappeared and the full beauty of the ruins in their setting became apparent. It has been a great favourite for painters.

CONWY FROM BENARTH
This picture is in brown ink and water-colour. The distant hills (across the Conwy Estuary) are all in shades of blue, while the castle is a rich reddish brown. The silhouette of the town needed shortening and simplifying a little. The whole thing has an autumn warmth about it and as the evening drew on, great shadows from the hill behind lengthened across the foreground fields.

CONWY CASTLE, page 38
It is interesting to compare the two Edwardian Castles of Conwy and Caernarfon. I still cannot make up my mind which I prefer. Many days were spent drawing them both from all sorts of positions and I would willingly do so again. The figures on the shore are my family and a French friend. On the right can be seen a portion of the great tubular bridge, designed by Robert Stephenson (son of George) that carried the new railway line to Holyhead. See how he added to the visual beauties of the Castle; a castellated gateway, followed by a walled embankment to carry the line along the base of the castle. To build it in a lighter stone was a stroke of genius — not for him to try to disguise his work, and to pretend to be mediæval. It was built in 1845 — twenty years or so after Telford's Suspension bridge, which can just be seen beyond the other.

PLASAU DUON, CLATTER, POWYS
Having made many journeys to central Wales in search of scenes to draw, I was struck by the many half-timbered houses to be found there, especially in the former County of Montgomery. An old friend and historian of this area suggested this particular house and a lovely subject it is, half way up the hillside looking down a valley not far from Newtown. Hundreds of years old — it is now a busy farmhouse with a courtyard filled with the sounds of squealing pigs and barking dogs. Wild Wales lies all around.

TREMADOG, page 41
A dignified but improbable "model village" all designed-as-a-piece, with a Market Place, cross in centre, Town Hall behind Hotel on the left and the great wall of the mountain for back cloth.

PENMON PRIORY, ANGLESEY, page 41
Penmon Priory has a hoary look about it, bleached and weathered by aeons of storms and the curious dome shaped building on the left is an enormous dovecot — similarly bleached by sun wind and rain. I had a great deal of trouble with a barbed wire fence here, placed to prevent sheep from falling down into a crevasse. I do so loathe barbed wire!

41

BEDDGELERT
A highly picturesque view of a famous and beautiful village, on the river Glaslyn. The drawing is carried out entirely in pencil and charcoal.

DINORWIC SLATE QUARRY, ELIDIR FAWR, page 42
When staying once with my wife and family at Caernarfon, we saw this remarkable scene before climbing Mount Snowdon — I decided to make a drawing of it. There being no public transport from Caernarfon, I got up early three or four mornings running and walked the six miles to get here at 8.30 a.m., for the morning light. Very exciting it was indeed to draw all the terraces, each showing their vertical shadows which grew longer or shorter, as the form of the mountain dictated. An explosion is taking place behind the pile of debris to the left of Llyn Peris.

   The road in the foreground runs from Caernarfon to Capel Curig and Llangollen and the view-point, is at the foot of Mount Snowdon itself. Soon after our visit, the Quarry was closed and adapted to a scheme for making electricity by raising the water of the lake each night and pouring it down again by day.

MONTGOMERY

We came upon this endearing scene quite by chance when driving to Harlech from England. Although Montgomery was once the capital of a county, it now seems remote and with very few inhabitants. So rare is a visitor that I was stoned by children who seemed to consider me a menace. Fortunately I was able to protect the drawing.

On the other hand the Doctor, who spoke to me day by day, said the picture must stay in Montgomery. So he bought it.

LLANGOLLEN, page 45

Everything that has been said and written extolling the delights of Llangollen is true in my opinion. The hills, the groups of trees and above all, the rocks in the river give the greatest visual pleasure. The town itself has little beauty. It was here that George Borrow spent much time with his wife and daughter before setting off on his great walk through Wales (for he was the worlds first 'hiker'). For a picture of what rural life was like in Wales more than a hundred years ago I give it full marks. It is a 'must' for all who visit Wales.

LLANIDLOES, Market Hall and Great Oak Street, page 45

I first came here in 1975 to draw the half-timbered Market Hall, which I had seen in an old pamphlet published by the Great Western Railway. It appeared to me so fascinating that I drew it from here and here and here . . . nearly boxing the compass in the process.

It is inevitable that when one sits for hours and days on a camp stool in the main street of a town or village, that one will make friends. And so it happened here. A lady spoke to me just as a lorry went by so that I could not hear, nor could I rise from my stool, as I had become stiff. . .So she knelt down, the better for me to hear, and this certainly made me stand up — for never had a lady knelt down to me! I could not approve! The message was that the lady and her husband were to open a shop in a few days time and could I let them have my work to frame and sell? So I did and they have been doing so ever since. Mavis and Michael Leopold are their names. Mr. Leopold is an absolute genius at making frames — he frames all the work I do of Welsh subjects.

LLANIDLOES, Church and River

The river Severn (Afon Haffron) here passes by the Church of Llanidloes where the banks have just been strengthened by gabions. The western tower is of such Welsh design that it could be nowhere else. In the distance the Long Bridge carries the road over the river to climb the mountains and wind its way over to Machynlleth.

To obtain this view (which I knew existed if only I could cross the river) was a labour: It was necessary to clamber over rocks, double up and press one's way through a wood, dense and thick and finally squat upon a rock and peer under overhanging leaves. Nonetheless the view was worth the effort.

CAERNARFON CASTLE AND THE RIVER SEIONT, LOW TIDE
A study of mud and water in the harbour at Caernarfon. No doubt most people would
prefer the water to be high, but I love the sinuous lines of the mud banks fashioned by
the never ending action of river and sea, wind and tide, always changing and always
beautiful. The lighting in this drawing is late afternoon. The Castle always flies two flags,
the Welsh Dragon and the Union Jack.

CAERNARFON CASTLE, QUEEN ELEANOR'S GATEWAY

The theme of this picture is the striking contrast between the small white, typically Welsh stone houses and the immense walls of the great Edwardian Castle. The building on the left is the Harbour-Master's Office, which, with the tall telephone pole give a splendid ending to that side of the picture. This is the only time I've used a telegraph pole as an essential part of a picture's composition.

CAERPHILLY CASTLE, MID-GLAMORGAN

I have an affinity with Caerphilly, for, in the twenties, when I was mad about railways, the first of the famous 'Castle' class of express locomotives was built at Swindon, by the Great Western Railway, and named *Caerphilly Castle*. I made a model of the locomotive (gauge "00") which I still have.

As this Castle (second in size in the kingdom for only Windsor covers a larger area) is in the centre of the town, the people have the finest City Centre one can possibly imagine, for one cannot shop, visit one's bank or go to the post office, without being cheered by the sight of antique towers, waving flags and sparkling water, with a background of hills and valleys.

NORTHUMBRIA

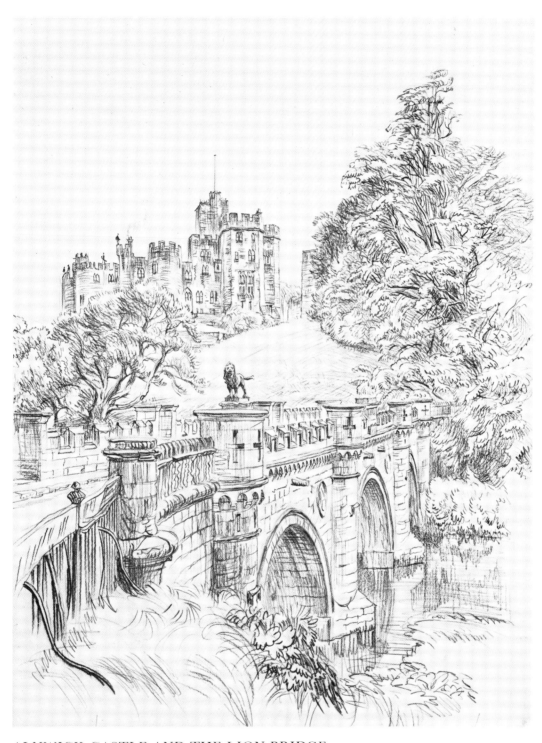

ALNWICK CASTLE AND THE LION BRIDGE

The bristling battlements of the Percy stronghold look down on the old Great North Road. A pencil sketch of Alnwick Castle that was going to be a water-colour.

Until a few years ago this bridge carried the Great North Road across the little river Aln. It stands at an angle at the bottom of a long hill between high stone walls, and is therefore the scene of many accidents. I was told by a man who chatted with me that he had never known more than a few weeks when there was not *some* damage to the stonework. Occasionally, the Lion is in the river! The main road now by-passes the town and castle.

Turner painted a beautiful water-colour from near here. He pushed his way along rough ground for a hundred yards to the right — then looked back and painted the bridge at right angles with the castle above and beyond, and all by moonlight. A marvellous, exquisite water-colour.

SALMON FISHING ON THE TWEED

Norham Castle, a great frontier stronghold was among Turner's favourite subjects. The trees would have horrified a mediæval constable of the castle which used to stand stark and bold against the Scots.

BERWICK-UPON-TWEED, page 52

England's most northerly town since 1482 with more scheduled buildings in proportion to its size than any other in England, among them the walls are thought to have anticipated the designs of the great French engineer, Vauban.

There are four versions of this subject but I like this one best. Apart from the Old Bridge the Town Hall, the Church and the lordly River Tweed, I was intrigued by the collection of statues and busts standing around in the foreground — Robert the Bruce and other Scottish worthies, and a Roman-looking head in bas relief from a bridge taken down some years ago. They mark the beginning of a long monumental mason's yard along a road that leads to Tweed Dock, in which there are usually to be found Dutch or Scandinavian ships discharging and taking on various commodities. The mason himself delighted in growing enormous leeks.

NORHAM CASTLE

The imposing view of the Keep of Norham Castle with its surrounding trees. It was in the field on the right when my wife and I saw an animal we could not give a name to. Was it a sheep or a goat? (it was in fact a Jacob's sheep). I relished the shadows cast by the fence rising in steps, a very nice piece of rural carpentering.

NORHAM

The village green at Norham, with the Castle in the background. The weathervane on top of the village cross is a salmon showing how highly the inhabitants regard this lordly fish. The place is wholly built of stone, and lies between the bridge and the castle which was one of Edward I's forward castles for "hammering the Scots".

BYWELL CASTLE AND THE RIVER TYNE

In February 1981, Bruce Allsopp, my good friend and publisher of this book, telephoned and said "Come up and stay with us here and draw Bywell Castle, just down the road". So, a month later I did just that having already decided to spend a part of April (that most glorious month!) drawing the Abbeys on the Scottish Border — and this is on the way.

The road crosses the Tyne by a monumental bridge designed in the grand manner: a few hundred yards downstream from the Castle. One clambers down to the riverside, here festooned with branches of trees torn down by the winter storms and floods, caught up by the rocks and boulders and young willows and alders, and then tries to find a spot giving a view across to the Castle. Occasionally I had to step onto a rock out in the river, in order to be clear of the branches, and to get a good study of the water.

ALNMOUTH

Another view which can be seen from the train between London and Edinburgh — what an inexhaustible series of subjects this journey has given me since my first in 1942! But it was more than twenty years later that I actually alighted at Alnmouth station, which was then the junction for the Alnwick branch, now alas, shut.

A walk along a few fields and a few jumps over rocks, the ubiquitous barbed wire and here was I with all this beauty spread before me. Violet blue sea, yellow sands, harbour filling and unfilling and the tide coming in and out, in the distance the Farne Islands myriads of birds, smoke from the houses, and a vehicle or two crossing the landward bridge and every half hour or two a train flew past, with passengers reading or talking, blissfully unaware of the beauties they were missing. But perhaps some did look.

NEWCASTLE UPON TYNE

When the great Hugo Wortham (the renowned "Peterborough" of the *Daily Telegraph*) reviewed the very first exhibition of my work, held at Messrs Colnaghi's in 1947, he wrote "when he adopts the grand manner he reminds one of Piranesi". But I had not then even heard of Piranesi! When I did see and study his work I was astonished and could scarcely accept the compliment. I mention the incident now however, for this scene in Newcastle upon Tyne (my favourite industrial town) looking across the deep gorge of the Tyne from Gateshead, is a true Piranesian subject. Nothing in Rome would have taxed one's capacities more. The Church (now Cathedral) and Castle, one behind the other, the Moot Hall, water-side buildings, the flowing river with a structure to carry the swing bridge in the centre, cast shadows falling on different surfaces, to mention but a few of the objects. Add to this the steep and stern perspective of the double-decker bridge, lit by sun and darkened by shadow, with a rough and dilapidated cobbled chare leading the eyes down into the picture and the smoke from the steam locomotive crossing the bridge, all add up to make a rare and dramatic scene. Newcastle abounds in such scenes.

NEWCASTLE, GREY STREET

My other drawing is more peaceful, less industrial and more elegant. It is of one of the finest streets in Europe, by name, Grey Street, and is perhaps the happiest result of all that early town planning carried out by Grainger and Dobson in the early 19th century on the higher levels of the city. The street rises gently and curves a little, its façades splendid in their noble designs and reaches a central point where stands the Grey Monument, a Doric column raised in honour of the father of the Reform Act of 1832. My picture is taken from a point in the gutter, just below the monument, showing the Theatre Royal; the stunning façade of the Bank of England, according to Pevsner, Dobson's crowning work, but now known to have been designed in Grainger's office. It has a long row of giant attached Corinthian columns. Nearer the spectator and just behind the group of figures on the island is the Turk's Head, an old and famous coaching Inn on the Great North Road. That too had a new façade built onto it in the Grainger and Dobson era. Just topping the roofs, midway, the Cathedral lantern can be seen.

DURHAM, with Framwellgate Bridge: Girtin's view
This is such a beautiful scene that it leaves me little to say. The picture is substantially the
same as it was 180 years ago when Girtin and Turner painted it. Some of the houses are
new (but nicely done) and one or two on the other side have been sensitively rebuilt,
keeping to the same modest dimensions. I like the scene best when the trees are *not* green.
There is an arch high overhead which carries the new by-pass across the river.

DURHAM, from Prebend's Bridge, page 60
Once again, words fail me. In Durham; we have perhaps the most beautiful City in the
kingdom, for it is the combination of noble architecture, both ecclesiastic and civic, with a
piece of topography teeming with those picturesque details so dear to the early romantics.
   Those who *must* see this particular view everyday are the boys of Durham School and
the students of the University.

DURHAM CATHEDRAL AND CASTLE, now the University, from above the Railway Station (for railway enthusiasts the engine is an N.E.R. 4–6–0 on a train from Newcastle to Liverpool).

DURHAM, Snow
Early on a Sunday morning looking out of a Norman window in the Judges' Quarters in
the Keep of the Castle, otherwise used as part of the University of Durham. A delicious
subject. While the day went on the Cathedral appeared and disappeared, as the snow
thinned and thickened and the sun shot out a ray or two now and then. Footsteps in the
snow are *perfect* for compositional purposes!

DURHAM, ELVET BRIDGE

WARKWORTH CASTLE, from the River Coquet
This is a famous view but I prefer it in winter. We had already experienced our first
snow, but it had melted when I arrived after a long bus ride from Newcastle (changing at
Ashington). The figure on the path was my landlady, exercising her Chihuahua: this was
so small I substituted a child.

DURHAM, ELVET BRIDGE, page 64
It was the reflections that really caused this drawing to come into existence: and also
because the bridge had a house built on it, that looked very attractive.
    Behind me, as I worked, was the great tree-clad hill upon which the Castle and
Cathedral are reared, so that, had I walked under the bridge and looked back, another
magnificent view of Durham would have presented itself. I shall do this one day.

YORKSHIRE AND LANCASHIRE

YORK, West Front by Night

The man who designed the West Front of York Minster should be canonised, and if he has not been, let him be so. His name is Master Simon and he was working in the early part of the 14th century, and died in 1322. The curvilinear window is generally considered the best ever conceived and carried out.

    As to the drawing, it is all in carbon pencil. There was a convenient lamp on the corner of the Purey-Cust Nursing Home above my left shoulder. One night it was out so I held a torch in my right hand. (I am left-handed). The greatest difficulty was turning out after supper and working away until midnight.

YORK, The Minster from Aldwark
Until recently, slums and derelict buildings filled the foreground here but a few years ago,
as part of the Lord Esher's suggestions for the future of York, the idea was put forward
that new houses should be built here and families live again within the walls of York.

   The well-known firm of Shepherds Homes, using the proper brick and red tiles, built the
houses and just as they had finished, I came again to York and was delighted to find this
new view. The very redness of the new tiles, together with the whiteness of the Minster
(it has recently been cleaned) made this scene one of great joy.

YORK, from the roof of the Mansion House, page 68
The Minster dominates all in this view of York from the roof of the Mansion House.

   Everyone's idea of a mediæval city, full of narrow streets, houses and shops, punctuated
here and there by the towers and spires of secondary churches, while below, lots of little
people, hurrying about their business, and above and beyond grand and beautiful, broods
an enormous Minster. I have drawn it four times, between 1942 and 1981 — but each
one has been done from a slightly different point of view. I must here acknowledge my
indebtedness to a succession of Lord Mayors, but also to my very old friend Mr. Charles
Minter, the City Engineer during the War, who first took me up there, when German
bombers had burned the mediæval Guildhall, now happily rebuilt, which stands just
behind.

FOUNTAINS ABBEY, SURPRISE VIEW

Ward Lock's guide to Harrogate said of Fountains Abbey and Studley Royal (in whose park it stands) *"is not a place to be scamped, and the visitor is strongly recommended to allow not less than four hours"* Four weeks, I'd say, or more...

Do not go by car or coach to the West end, but go from Ripon to the little village of Studley Roger that stands about the gates to the Park of Studley Royal and then walk up the long long drive and so down to the first lake and through more gates. Then you continue through the pleasure grounds, enormous yew hedges with glimpses here and there of lakes and temples, gorgeous woods hang about your head for you are now in a narrow valley; a turn or two and where the path divides take the upper one and in a short time you find a simple summer house on your left, and there is the Abbey with the river running down from it to a great half-moon pond which lies far below.

THE RUINS OF FOUNTAINS ABBEY, page 71
The Nave looking West, drawn on summer evenings from 6p.m. until dusk.

MEDIÆVAL MILL, FOUNTAINS ABBEY, page 71
It was the winter trees that caused me to make this drawing. I cannot resist them, but the temperature limits time spent. The building with buttresses is the 13th century corn mill belonging to Fountains Abbey which has been used until quite recently. It stands in rather a remote part of the area and is not noticed by many of those who come and admire.

Dennis Flanders April 1943

Dennis Flanders March 1944

71

FOUNTAINS, Surprise View from below, (see page 70)
Some of the matchless beauty drawn and painted in the quiet of the sunny June
mornings, the River, the Skell it is called, drops down a little dam and begins to form the
half-moon pond. As I recall the days I smell again the fresh aroma of wild garlic.

CASTLE BOLTON, Wensleydale
A very different scene. Painted during the war in one day (a Sunday) on a forty-eight
hour pass with my particular friend James Porteous Wood. We cycled the 25 miles from
Ripon the night before.
   Castle Bolton was for many years the home of the very much loved painter Fred
Lawson, whose daughter Sonia carries on the good work.

RIPON CATHEDRAL, The Chapter House
Here in this Norman Chapter House, Dean Birchenough instructs a girl in preparation for
Confirmation. The round windows are a very beautiful feature echoing the interlacing ribs
of the vaults.

RIPON, Market Place and Cathedral, page 74
This wide view of Ripon was from the roof of Messrs Montague Burton's Tailoring
Establishment. During the war years the upper floor was a canteen and a short flight of
stairs led to this stunning vista. The plain of York lies in the distance.
   On the far right is the Georgian Town Hall with its proud motto "Except the Lord
Keep the City, the Wakeman wakest in vain", which refers, of course, to the Wakeman
himself, a city dignitary who blows a curfew horn each evening, from the steps of the
Monument, to the North, to the South, to the East and to the West.
   The shop with the sun-blind down is Harrison's Bookshop. My copy of *The Dalesman*
that marvellous monthly about Dales life that I have taken since 1948 still comes through
Harrison's Bookshop. It began long before Heriot was ever thought of!

STAITHES, Looking out to Sea
Staithes was made famous by the publication of the autobiography of the painter Dame Laura
Knight during the thirties and Captain Cook worked in a shop here when he was a boy. The
combination of closely built cottages standing almost one on top of another; the stern lines of the
tall stratified cliffs, and the long paralleled lines of the rocky beach all make up a picture of a wild
and inhospitable coast line.

STAITHES, The Village and the Shore, page 76
The Yorkshire coast is unexpectedly full of colour, much more so, in my opinion, than that of
Cornwall. There is nothing of the greyness of the North here. The cliffs are red, yellow brown and
purple with long lines of dark granite along the shore when the tide is out. As you see in the picture
the cottages are all sorts of colours with bright pantile roofs. The cliff face on the right was a puzzle
to draw especially as each recess threw its own shadow and the sun goes round so quickly.

CARTMEL PRIORY, FURNESS

Another composition essentially built up of triangles. This is an autumn scene, with the centre trees yellow and crimson. Cartmel is a comely town and I made this drawing, when staying at a house nearby, a Methodist Guest House known as Abbot Hall which wanted some pictures for postcards. You have to sing a hymn before eating, and there were glorious views across Morecambe Bay.

MIDDLEHAM. WENSLEYDALE

That much maligned English King, Richard III spent much of his time in this great castle, the mighty seat of the powerful family of Nevilles and here he met his wife, the Lady Ann, and spent much of the happiest years of his life here. It was the "Windsor" to his Northern capital of York. Now it has been called the "Newmarket" of the North, due to the large number of horse-training stables in the vicinity.

I tried to draw the castle from outside the village but the wastes of snow were absolutely baleful and made outside work impossible. But in a room over the bar of an inn, with stable lads for company at meals, and an oil stove to keep me warm, I spent a happy few days drawing this small Wensleydale town.

BOLTON PRIORY AND THE ROOFS OF BOLTON HALL

Scenes of roofs and chimneys have always exercised a fascination for me, especially when seen from above. In the centre of this scene is the famous and beautiful Bolton Priory, half ruin, half parish church. It stands by the river Wharfe and we have been fortunate enough to stay at the Rectory nearby with the late Rev. Tomlinson and his charming family. The gatehouse of the Priory was turned into a hunting lodge after the Dissolution. It was much favoured, by King George V.

When we stayed with the Rector, whose Parish was far-flung we witnessed a style of living that was passing. Morning call was a hymn-tune rung by the Rector on bells. After assembling at our chairs in the dining room he would read a chapter from the Bible, then after a great scraping of chairs, family and guests alike knelt down and prayers were said; after which Mrs. Tomlinson brought in a huge bowl of hot porridge.

The view from the dining room window was a real picture itself — a waterfall, stepping stones across the Wharfe, a cliff, distant woods and far to the south the huge shape of Ilkley Moor.

BARDEN TOWER
If I had to choose one drawing that showed all the stern beauty of architecture in the
Yorkshire Dales, it would be this. It is of Barden Tower, a few miles north of Bolton
Abbey in Wharfedale.

RICHMOND, THE MARKET-PLACE

This seems to me to be a good example of what the centre of a town should look like. The Castle Keep stands lofty but retired. Without it, the town would never have been built. Then you have the great market-place and scattered about in orderly array; houses, shops, the Parish Church, and a monument with lamps and steps for people to sit on — to have a rest and a chat before continuing their business. As you see, the square, is still cobbled, though there are tarmac pathways linking up salient points. One rather sad loss took place recently; a few shops that had been built up against the church were removed — such a pity!

HORNBY CASTLE AND VILLAGE, LANCASHIRE, page 82

This is high up in Lunedale, where the Wenning comes down to join the more famous river Lune. The Castle (like one of King Ludwig's in Bavaria) stands on a height between the two streams. It dates from the early 16th century and has been converted into several handsome residences.

I made the drawing from an embankment of the disused railway line from Skipton to Lancaster. This gave me a higher vantage point to see more of the beautiful Pennine mountains behind. On the left is the octagonal tower of the church, and along the road near the foreground is the bus returning to Lancaster.

SELBY

A bright and breezy morning in early spring by the waterside at Selby. (It snowed now and then). I took a great fancy to this place. It is not "tarted up", at all, as tourists are not really supposed to go to Selby! The river rises and falls, a loud clatter from the left, as trains cross over the lines of the swing bridge, a huge barge slowly creeps silently by and lorries, cars, cycles, pedestrians, constantly pass the other bridge, but oneself is left in peace on the grassy bank. I took great pleasure in dealing with the water — some extraordinary colours were observed as the sun shone on the not-so-clean water, a wind dapple here and there and a breeze that kept on altering the flow of the water.

BEVERLEY, SATURDAY MARKET-PLACE

I sat mostly in the gutter to make a picture of this beautiful market-place because there were so many shoppers and passers-by, as of course, was normal.

A very fine broad market-place, full of interesting items. The most prominent is the Market Cross which is a perfect work of art in itself. The local guide tells you who gave it to the town but not who designed it, which is of much greater importance. Pillars, cupola, coats of arms, exquisitely wrought and beautifully maintained, are a delight to the eye. It is a great pity that so many cars hem it in. Behind, you can see the imposing, Wensleydale-cheese-coloured tower of St Mary's Church which, though not so famous as Beverley Minster, is very fine.

ROCHDALE

It is always a great pleasure to visit a town that is never considered to be a tourist
paradise. Rochdale is such a one and here is a picture of it, showing all the elements of
the picturesque. In the distance is the church on an eminence of its own. The tower is
that of the stunning Town Hall, as good as any in Flanders . . . The curve in the street is
a delight and so are the people. The little cat was waiting for a car to come and park and
when it did, it sat on the roof. Memories of Gracie Fields and "The Biggest Aspidistra in
the World!".....

DONCASTER, LOCOMOTIVE WORKS, page 86

Here is a scene we shall never see again, but a subject I had wanted to draw for years. It
is of the rebuilding shed at the LNER works at Doncaster. All the engines are Gresley
Pacifics being rebuilt. This drawing was one of a series I made of Yorkshire industries for
publication in *The Yorkshire Post* in which Sir Linton Andrews, the editor, became
interested. The trouble was that I thought of it in July instead of December, so all these
drawings of wool sheds, ship-building berths etc., were done in the heat of summer
instead of the cool of winter which would have been much more sensible!

KNARESBOROUGH

This is a happy picture painted with my particular friend James Porteous Wood, both of us sitting in a punt, fixed at right angles to the bank, so that we were able to dip our brushes in the river, what bliss! It was a July evening and many folk were out on the water punting up and down the beautiful river Nidd.

ROTHERHAM

An old photograph showing a dilapidated and broken down old bridge at Rotherham with a chapel on it seemed to me to hold possibilities for a picture, so when, years later, I found myself staying at Bakewell, as a base for making drawings of both Chatsworth House and Haddon Hall, and furthermore finding that there was a bus at 9 a.m. to Sheffield, I toyed with the idea of taking a day off to visit Rotherham, which I knew was not far beyond.

The journey from Sheffield to Rotherham was as dreary as that from Birmingham to Wolverhampton. But as I stood on the bridge at Rotherham and looked up and saw the church, I realised that Rotherham was an old town with a heart.

Now the church was on a hill, I was on the old bridge, beautifully restored I noticed, and the chapel as well, so I looked eagerly the other way along the small river Rother to find whether perchance there was some window or flat roof from which I could make a picture, using the bridge in the middle and the church beyond. Yes, there was such a flat roof. After a good deal of trouble, I found it was the back part of a Workmen's Club so I went in (it was like a big pub) and spoke to the barman. When I said I was an artist, he thought I was an *artiste* wanting a job — but all was settled amicably and in an hour after my arrival in Rotherham I was on that flat roof and working hard.

ST MARY'S, LANCASTER
The approach to the great Church of Lancaster, with the felicitously placed beech tree, just at the right angle.
On the left is part of the Castle Wall, now H.M. Prison.

LIVERPOOL TOWN HALL

One of a suite of rooms of matchless beauty through which it is possible endlessly to walk since they are arranged in a rectangle around a superlative staircase. They are composed of a great ballroom, a dining room, small ante-room, and a series of reception rooms.

The style is that of James Wyatt, who however had a remarkable assistant called John Foster, a local man, and many famous furniture designers added the works of their genius. The colouring of these rooms is rich and splendid indeed; white, gold, green, yellow, Siena pilasters and maroon damasked curtains; also (and to me unique) a whole series of tall stoves, richly ornamented, flanked by clusters of lamps and fitted into alcoves. Liverpool is indeed a wonderful city.

LANCASTER

A fine composition, the Castle and Church crowning the hill and encircled by the river at its base. The handsome bridge was designed by Thomas Harrison at the end of the 18th century and is said to be the first of its kind in this country, on which the roadway is level, instead of rising and falling as is usual. Compare old Waterloo Bridge in London and Kelso Bridge over the Tweed. A little further upstream is another similar bridge only this time it is an aqueduct and is by John Rennie himself, a few years later than the road bridge.

LIVERPOOL CATHEDRAL

In my notes about Liverpool Town Hall I mentioned John Foster, as one of the designers. He was a Liverpool man, a surveyor and a dock engineer, and in 1827 he created the great St James's Cemetery from a disused stone quarry, partly by building great cyclopæan walls to contain the sides and arches for catacombes. This has made a magnificent foreground for the superb Cathedral by Sir Giles Gilbert Scott OM, RA, that stuns the visitor into silence while its full majesty sinks into the soul. It is built of glowing pink sandstone.

In this picture you can see how I have enjoyed framing the building with the old bushes and trees. I remember the weather was a little misty which made all the stone even more pink and the shadows more blue. I had recently been in France, drawing Albi Cathedral and could not help feeling that Scott had it in mind when he thought out his design for Liverpool. I have since learned that he did.

SOUTH AND EAST
FROM THE PEAK

PEVERIL CASTLE AND THE PEAK CAVERN GORGE, DERBYSHIRE

There are many wonderful scenes in the Peak District and I am very conscious that my work there is of the slightest. But here at least is something very dramatic and worthy of the deepest study in romantic scenery. Peveril Castle tops the hill and a great crack in the mountainside stops even trees from finding a foothold.

At the bottom is the famous Peak Cavern at the entrance to which stands the entrancing village of Castleton, all built of stone. The original is a coloured drawing, mostly green and grey. The farmer, his geese and his cows make a typical foreground.

HADDON HALL, near Bakewell
As a neighbour of Chatsworth, Haddon Hall could not be more dissimilar. It is a romantic castellated manor-house which has grown through the centuries, much 'improved' with Gothic style additions and restored in 1912. Superbly sited above a handsome old bridge over the river Wye it contains some beautiful rooms, the best on the south side overlooking a terrace and formal gardens.

BAKEWELL
A charming market town in the Peak District on the river Wye; it makes a convenient centre to study the two great houses of Chatsworth and Haddon Hall and all the splendid country around. The church is beautiful and worthy of a good number of drawings because of its dramatic situation on a steep hill, with mountains all around.

As I was drawing, a coach and four horses merrily bowled over the bridge. The passengers, both inside and out raised hats and smiled and the driver raised his whip and the guard blew his horn with great vigour and myself bowed in answer . . . A most unusual occurrence!

CEDARS AT CHATSWORTH

The sides of the valley of the Derwent are of blue hills, the floor is of green grass, the buildings are of grey stone, houses, walls and barns. Here is a distant view of Chatsworth House, that Palace of the Peak, set between two glorious cedars that were a sheer joy to draw. You can see the river below and that strange squarish mass of stone in the centre, is a part of a folly called "Queen Mary's Bower".

Chatsworth is the principal seat of the Dukes of Devonshire.

BASLOW

The estate of Chatsworth contains within its boundaries, several villages, Beeley, Edensor, Baslow and Nether End. The river winds its way between the sides of the Dale. Here you see the attractive church of Baslow set close beside the water, with its accompanying trees, just about to burst out in leaf, for it is early April.

THE GLORY HOLE, LINCOLN
Nothing particular happened when rendering this attractive scene in Lincoln, except, I remember, it was one of the early days of that extremely hot summer we had in 1976. On this morning the sun was very bright and for the first time in England, I noticed a shadow on the water, such as one frequently sees in Southern Europe.

LINCOLN, THE POTTER GATE

Another favourite subject of the early water-colourists. Peter de Wint painted it many times for he finally lived at Lincoln — he had come up to stay with a friend from the Royal Academy. He liked it and his friend's sister so he married her and lived there happily ever after.

In this picture the thing to enjoy is the way the building seems to lean backwards so as not to slip down the hill — for it is a fearful hill.

Dennis Flanders Lincoln

Dennis Flanders

LINCOLN FROM BRAYFORD POOL

This is another favourite view of that great Cathedral of Lincoln, showing the splendour of its position, comparable to that of Durham. There is an animated water-foreground and a fine group of old warehouses with overhanging storeys for the loading and unloading of stores. But to see it now, you will have a shock. The tree on the island has gone as have the commercial barges at the mooring posts. The warehouses have been denuded of their overhanging upper storeys. A main road has been driven across the middle shore and the water is filled with plastic yachts with plastic pennants beating incessantly against plastic masts. But the water is still there and so is the Cathedral, and the sun still shines.

LINCOLN, THE CATHEDRAL AND EXCHEQUER GATE, page 102

This is one of the great classic views of England, which I have had the pleasure of drawing many times. The foreground is known as Castle Square.

It would be presumptious for me to comment upon the towers of the Cathedral, each time I draw them the labour becomes a sort of prayer to beauty.

In this case, my idea was to set the towers back and contrast this delicacy with the steep, dark perspective of the half-timbered house on the left. Late afternoon shadows creep across the gateway and the backs of cars finish off the composition.

BOSTON MARKET-PLACE

St. Botolph's, the great tower of which dominates not only the town but miles of countryside, not to mention the vast expanses of the Wash. I have seen the 'Stump' (as it is called locally) from the Norfolk side of the mouth of the Ouse beyond King's Lynn. Here, however in the first picture, is the Market-Place, where, as you see, it is Market Day and, just above one of the distant stalls, near the East End of the church, is a statue. It commemorates Sir Herbert Ingram, founder of *The Illustrated London News*, a local boy who certainly made good. It was under his grandson Sir Bruce, who edited the paper for 60 years, and the latter's nephew, Hugh Ingram, that I worked for eight years, joining those artists whose work had graced the paper for more than 100 years.

BOSTON. High Tide after Sundown. July

This is the usual view of Boston taken by both photographers and artists (I met Sir Henry Rushbury drawing it one day in the fifties) and so decided not to draw it. But, during my visit there in mid-summer sometime during the sixties I was walking to another spot after supper to get in another hour's work on a river subject, when I happened to turn round and look backwards. This hackneyed view was transformed. The sun had gone down beneath the horizon and the sky was lemon yellow, a cyanine blue at the zenith and the church tower was purple. The other building had a weird glow and all the shadows were deepening, while the water, being at high tide was absolutely still and reflecting the lemon sky by a deeper lemon colour. I stood transfixed and tried to take it all in, in case tomorrow was raining. In any case the tide would be lower. Oh! the difficulties of drawing tidal subjects over a period of days. However, I drew the picture during subsequent days and partially remembered the colours. This experience was an object lesson in the importance of lighting in a picture.

BOSTON, warehouses from the roof of the cinema

One of the most interesting features of Boston (as at King's Lynn and Wisbech) are the large number of warehouses that line the river bank and harbours, built, I believe mostly in the early 19th century and often now derelict. Strenuous efforts are being made for finding uses for them (here the further one is now a music school and centre and beautifully restored. But some have been demolished. I was determined to find a composition using these splendid roof tops as well as the sublime tower of St Botolph's; and the roof of the cinema seemed the spot.

The façade of Fydell house can be seen in the bottom right hand corner. This was the town house of a ... and now a part of Nottingham University.

THE CORN EXCHANGE, LOUTH
I had a room at an inn here, while drawing a house in the neighbourhood, and I spent
the hours after dinner making this drawing of the fine old Corn Exchange by night. You
can see the spire of the church dimly in the background.

It is a fascinating exercise in shadows going upwards instead of the usual
downwards.

FOTHERINGHAY

This magnificent church, fit for a Cathedral, is all that is left of a chantry and a college
— a castle and a palace — and the charming village of Fotheringhay with its bridge over
the Welland. Its fame was assured when Mary Queen of Scots, after six months
imprisonment, was beheaded there. After that the castle and college seem to have been
abandoned and now only the torso of the church, a mound once the base of the castle and
a pretty village remain. All the rest is deepest, rural Northamptonshire.

NEWARK, BRIDGE AND CHURCH, page 108

The river is the Trent and the church in the background is one of the grandest in
England, and can be compared to those of Grantham and Louth not far away. The castle
is just seen on the extreme right. The half timbered building behind the striped wall on
the left is a fascinating structure known as the Ossington Coffee Tavern, given by a
daughter of the Duke of Portland in a desire to increase the habit of temperance.

The bridge has been somewhat spoiled by the erection of projecting walkways in
1881, but the treatment of the opposite river bank slopes, railings and steps is beautifully
managed. A few stalls are sometimes to be seen here.

The market-place — a rather large irregular rectangle is splendid. You have to see it
to believe it.

The Trent, is considered by many to mark the boundary between the North and the
South of England.

GREAT BARFORD, BEDFORDSHIRE
One of the long bridges that span the wide valley of the Ouse. This river floods very easily, thus most of the bridges have long causeways and extra arches to deal with such conditions. Many of the bridges are very old and very beautiful. Here at Great Barford is a happy combination of church, farm and bridge, built partly of brick and partly of stone.

THE GREAT OUSE AT HEMINGFORD GREY

This type of landscape abounds in Southern England and very lovely it is. This boathouse
and café are somewhat dilapidated and I believe one has collapsed. But the curve of the
river is still there and so is the church. It is frequently my habit to telephone a painter,
Stanley Orchart, who lives nearby and suggest a day out in the East Midlands. If he
agrees, I catch the first train to Huntingdon, where he picks me up and we go to some
delectable spot and instead of fishing we draw and paint.

SOUTHWELL MINSTER

This drawing is the result of a commission from a client who lives in Cambridge, for his wife who spent her childhood here and dearly loves the place. It is a village city, its Cathedral mediæval and full of most glorious things, while the feel of the place is comfortably Georgian.

Byron knew the place for his first lady-love, Mary Chaworth, lived here and his family home, romantic Newstead Abbey is not far away. The curious top to the Cathedral towers are so unusual (in England yes — not so in France) that they are the *motif* that sets the design of the drawing, which is made up of triangles. The churchyard gateway and the yew tree echo the tops of the towers — and who knows but that it was some gardener who decided the yew tree must do just that.

All was peace until the last day, when all the Boy scouts of Nottinghamshire came and had a grand parade up and down, right in front of my very eyes!

THE ROOFS OF WELBECK ABBEY, page 112

Welbeck is one of the great houses that adorn the district known as the Dukeries and their parks form what is, in effect, Sherwood Forest. I spent the last six months of my army career here, for it became Northern Command's Formation College where men and women not yet due for demobilisation, went to learn or re-learn their trades. The surroundings were sheer bliss and all sorts of wonderful things happened. Riding before breakfast for instance. I think more engagements and marriages were planned here than ever before.

This remarkable composition of the Virgin's Wing, as the long curved building is called, joins the two ancient Huntingdon Smithson buildings (1623–5) to the main house. One is the riding school, the other the chapel and library to the main house, on the roof of which I sat and made this drawing.

113

EAST ANGLIA

NORWICH, ST PETER MANCROFT
There are more than thirty old parish churches in Norwich the largest of which is St Peter Mancroft seen here across the busy market place. It is a splendid example of fifteenth century architecture and I drew it for *The Illustrated London News* while the roof was being repaired.

NORWICH CATHEDRAL

This beautiful Cathedral, is the brightest jewel in the beauteous crown of Norfolk
Churches. I chose to draw its West End in the evenings at the height of summer when the
sun had already passed the west and the shadows were falling from the north. The arch is
that of the Erpingham Gate which, as all arches do, has the effect of concentrating the eye
on the object beyond.

116

PETERBOROUGH CATHEDRAL AND MARKET-PLACE.

Half of Peterborough has recently been rebuilt but the Authorities have left this scene alone. We can still admire the Town Hall, its arches and the gateway to the Close screening the west front of the great Fenland Minster, whose turrets and gables appear above. It used to be called Medhampstead.

Go through the gateway and you will find the most splendid west front in the world — three enormous pointed archways rising up to the full height of the roof, whilst an elaborate porch, projects from the centre arch.

This drawing was being worked on late one July Sunday evening after a day spent sketching with Stanley Orchart by the River, away in the country. This was not quite his cup of tea, so he was mooching about poking here and there in order to find another subject to work on another day. Although a very fine-looking man with a full beard and a deep resonant voice, on a summer evening Sunday sketching among fields and river banks, he did not seem, shall I say, quite the elegant banker or stockbroker . . . as he was idly watching the Salvation Army (you see their banners and bonnets in my picture) he was asked (very kindly of course,) if he needed a bed for the night! How we laughed!

ST IVES

Until the obliteration of Huntingdonshire, St Ives was its second town. Now it has been absorbed into a larger Cambridgeshire. Here, the River Ouse, having traversed the whole of Bedfordshire from West to East, finally enters the Fens. This drawing was made in early Spring. The meadows were wet and everything was bright and breezy, with glorious skies but very cold.

BRAMPTON MILL NEAR HUNTINGDON
Still the River Ouse, it was these tall trees straining up to the sky and flinging their arms
aloft all standing around the old watermill that attracted me so much — and see how the
water pours down and out of the mill leat — tearing up all the reflections.

ELY, THE CATHEDRAL AND THE GALLERY
The remarkable western tower illuminated by the midday sun, while the Gallery (as the long range of mediæval buildings on the right is called), having been in shadow, gradually receives the sun as it moves over to the west.

ELY CATHEDRAL FROM PALACE GREEN

Ely, dominated by its remarkable Cathedral seems to attract me more and more as the years go by. It was the reading of Lord Lytton's *Hereward The Wake* that first sent me there (on a Sunday afternoon half-day excursion from Liverpool Street at 4/6d. and I've loved it ever since. Apart from Southwell in Nottinghamshire, Ely is the smallest Cathedral City in England.

Observe the high house on the left. Its roof exhibits to perfection the traditional method of mixing different coloured tiles. As near as I can observe some are red, others yellow and others yet again brown. How the builders arrange these in an equable fashion is a mystery to me, but the effect is charming, and particularly so, above the warm yellow ochre brick much favoured in this part of the country. Whole villages are built like this and also parts of Cambridge itself.

WISBECH, THE CRESCENT
This Norfolk town is full of surprises. For instance, one would not expect to find this crescent of houses which is nearly complete (but not quite). I was fascinated by the church clock which renders the hours difficult to understand. The metal circles which hold the numerals together and the hands project forward for a foot or so, each item thus throwing its shadowy impression upon the wall. The man is putting something in his dustbin while pussy is considering crossing the road. I always have the impression that there is less bustle and hustle in East Anglian towns than in other parts of the country.

KING'S LYNN, SATURDAY MARKET-PLACE, page 122
With one of the two western-towers of St Margaret's Church. The market stall looks very small I admit, but the Tuesday Market-Place is enormous and very animated. Sandringham is not far away and King's Lynn has a yearly Festival of the Arts, usually attended by a member of the Royal Family.

CAMBRIDGE, TRINITY STREET AND ST JOHN'S STREET, page 122
The combination of different buildings (all of them excellent of this kind) observed one sunny morning, gave me the idea that this scene was one of the finest in Cambridge. The two features that give it excitement are the arch of the bank in the left foreground and the trees on the right; so the curve of the street, Trinity Chapel, the entrance to St John's and its lovely tower behind, are all set off to perfection.

KING'S COLLEGE CHAPEL from the roof of The Copper Kettle restaurant

The drawing above, showing the exterior of the chapel, reminds one of another fact that had often occurred to me while contemplating choice examples of architecture. It is usually the case that it is *either* the exterior *or* the interior that gives the greater pleasure. In this case, however, it seems a miracle has been achieved, for both are equally splendid. The block on the left beyond the grass is a part of the Fellows' Building, built by James Gibbs; on the right in the distance is the Tower of St John's, while in front is the exquisite Senate House (also by Gibbs) with the perfectly placed chestnut tree in front. The foreground is occupied by Wilkins' splendid screen, which makes a perfect foil to the chapel itself.

CAMBRIDGE, interior of the Chapel of King's College, page 124

The splendour of this interior is almost overwhelming. Surely no other building in Britain shows more perfection. Its size, large enough to be infinitely impressive but not to dwarf humanity; its grace of line, its spaciousness, its stained-glass of which there is so much, and which paints the floor with its colour, as in the centre, reared up upon a dark screen — the glorious organ case with trumpeting angels, whose proportion to the whole is just right and the light of the sky pouring in from all sides.

NEWPORT, ESSEX
I wonder how many people travelling backwards and forwards from Liverpool Street to Cambridge, have *not* caught sight of this attractive Essex town. The nearest house is lavishly adorned with pargetting and has a very fine shell doorway. Of course, the poplar tree *makes* the picture and I'm not sure it still stands. One day, many years ago, I cycled from my home in Woodford and drew it.

PANFIELD HALL near Braintree, page 126
This house dates from 1545, and the tower was added later. Originally it was the hospital of a nearby Priory, of which only the name remains. Essex is one of the least known of the south eastern counties and contains many little known treasures, in the way of unspoilt villages, and country houses, which, being largely of modest size, are still lived-in and not open to the public. One such is Panfield. It is built of warm red brick, mellowed by time, and surrounded by well grown trees; a delight to draw. You can see behind, the farm buildings and the haystack, with a glimpse of the small church beyond.

WALCOT CHURCH, NORFOLK, page 126
In the far distance is a thin line of violet. It is the North Sea. Nearer a hint of a few buildings and then the churchyard wall and a field or two. The church (stone with flint knapping) with its dignified tower and on the left the barn and the farmhouse, bright red pantiles,, brown and white flint with red brick corners — a typical and beautiful Norfolk scene and a study in parallel lines.

CHEVINGTON HALL AND FARM, SUFFOLK
The perfection of the Suffolk scene. In the centre is Chevington Hall, a modest 17th century manor house-cum-farm. All around are signs of busy life — the pig pens, the open doors of the barns, the tyres of the tractors. Behind, trees give comfort and warmth to the site and behind everything is the tower of the modest church.

KIMBOLTON CASTLE, near Huntingdon, page 129
It is Sir John Vanburgh, that genius of an Architect, that gives a sense of drama to this great house. And look at the splendid avenue of Wellingtonias, all with their attendant shadows lying across the grass. It was once the home of the Dukes of Godmanchester, who have emigrated to Kenya and it is now a very fine school. But before that a great number of events took place in an older house and in the fine old town that stands at its gates. Queen Catherine of Aragon died here and the judge who condemned Sir Walter Raleigh lies buried in the church. He was of the Montagu family.

WISBECH, page 129
The broad river Nene, flowing between two rows of fine houses, makes this an unusual picture for an English market town, but quite irresistible. The roadways on either side of the water are known engagingly as the North Brink and the South Brink, those of the North seemingly superior to the South! The dark boat chugging along the river completes the picture — holds the two sides together and makes a focal point. Otherwise it is a difficult subject. Beyond the bend and out of the picture is the town bridge, followed by the docks, the warehouses, the market place, and a magnificent church.

FROM THE WELSH
BORDER TO LONDON

STOKESAY CASTLE AND CHURCH
This subject has haunted me with its weird beauty, more than any other I can remember. Beautiful and romantic it certainly is in full measure, yet there is an indefinable air of sadness about it.

CHESTER, THE CANAL
This astonishing sight was originally part of the Roman defences.

SHREWSBURY, WYLE COP

Now here is an urban scene *par excellence*. But the picture must be made before 10 a.m. in summer. If you come later, half of its charm is gone. The building on the right is the famous Lion Hotel and the beautiful half-timbered house with stained-glass windows is that in which Harry Tudor stayed before the battle of Bosworth, which ended the unhappy Wars of the Roses and installed the Tudors on the English throne. If you try to photograph this scene, you cannot. On the island is an enormous road sign at eye level, giving all sorts of unnecessary information. And, by the same token, Shrewsbury, beautiful as it is, has a dreadful system of one-way traffic that includes no pedestrian crossings (save one or two on the edges of the city) so as you shop or just walk about, you find yourself endlessly waiting to cross the road.

CHESTER, OLD DEE BRIDGE AND THE BRIDGEGATE
The Dee is tidal up to this point, which is shown here at the flood. At low tide the drop is remarkable to behold and as the water rises you can smell the sea. The famous Dee Mills stood just across the river — vast they were and prison-like. They were burned down in 1895.

CHESTER, CATHEDRAL AND CANAL
The Canal in Chester is in continuous use, and here you see one of the long boats passing under a new bridge which carries the inner ring road. I've told a visual lie here, for the arch is actually a rectangular opening. But it is a pity to spoil a picture just for someone else's lack of aesthetic sense!

SHREWSBURY, ST ALKMUND'S STEEPLE, THE BEAR STEPS AND
ST JULIAN'S CHURCH

Chester and Shrewsbury, though neighbouring county capitals, and both full of beauty
and interest, could hardly be more different. Shrewsbury is all hills, alleys, and spires,
whilst Chester is flat, calm and aloof. Here is Fish Street, partly restored, cobbles and all,
which the great Turner found irresistible.

SHREWSBURY, ST MARY'S ABBEY AND THE ENGLISH BRIDGE
Here is a study of the magnificent bridge that carries the Holyhead Road into
Shrewsbury. I have drawn it several times but prefer this sharp perspective view, done
after 5 p.m. on summer evenings. A narrow staircase leads down to the river and does not
give sufficient vision to see the bridge properly. I derived great help by drawing it from a
point diametrically opposite, as in a mirror, but of course, I had to change all the
shadows! The Abbey is of a beautiful rose-red colour.

MONMOUTH, MONNOW BRIDGE
This is such a fascinating building that I drew it three times, and would have enjoyed drawing it again. Here it is shown from downsteam, from the edge of a field full of caravans. There is glorious country all around Monmouth.

TINTERN, page 136
The great thing to do when you go to Tintern is to cross the river (by a curious iron bridge once carrying a quarry railway line) and enjoy the prospect of the Abbey, the woods and cottages of the small village, with the river in the foreground, which is tidal.

This is a very renowned beauty spot, much loved by Victorian travellers, by Wordsworth and by the great landscape painters. But I had just a hint of a feeling that the Department of the Environment in whose keeping it is, mean the visitor to stay on the road side of the river and not to explore the other bank.

MONMOUTH, AGINCOURT SQUARE

What a name! The statue in the niche in the centre of the Town Hall façade is that of Henry V, who was born in the castle here. The other figure (on the pedestal in front) represents Charles Stewart Rolls, one of the pioneers of aviation. But Monmouth is loved for the beauty of its situation among steep hills, the charm of its buildings, its long main street leading from the group of church, school and main square gently downhill to the Monnow Bridge at the bottom. Now in Wales it appears to be the perfect county town.

CHEPSTOW CASTLE, GWENT

Formerly in Monmouthshire, a border castle now in Wales The river is the Wye, so the
view-point is in England, Gloucestershire to be precise. This foreground seemed rather
soft, I found, and several of the inhabitants of the little houses you can see on the far
right of the picture were complaining to the Council that their gardens were about to be
swept away. The Castle is overpowering in its size and grandeur. You will see I have
some little sunbeams showing through the windows. The drawing is now hanging up in a
house at Aberystwyth.

Dennis Flanders.

GLOUCESTER

The lace-like tower of Gloucester Cathedral looks as if it were carved out of Wensleydale cheese, for its tone shows a pale lemon-like colour, quite unique in my experience. Here it is seen rising above some of the interesting buildings of the Close. On the right, the half-timbering is of the Parliament House, used as such on several occasions during the time of the Plantagenet Kings. In order to express my pleasure at the beauty of the tower, I have drawn it in lead pencil and show a shaft of sunshine shooting down, while the rest of the drawing is carried out in brown ink.

THE MONNOW GATE, MONMOUTH, page 140

This was a very impressive toll gate but capable of being defended, not really a town gateway.

STRATFORD-ON-AVON

It is a matter of amazement that this town, having been a place of pilgrimage to the shrine of Shakespeare for more than three hundred years, has remained so modest and unspoilt. It is still a remarkably beautiful old town.

Here in Chapel Street looking into Church Street are the dawn and evening scenes of the great poet's life. Between the left-hand house and the Guild Chapel is the site of Shakespeare's house, New Place, which hides a beautiful knot garden. Behind the Chapel is the Grammar School which he attended; while on the right is the old Falcon Hotel, which he probably knew well.

BIRMINGHAM, THE BULL RING, 1952

The grand old Parish Church of Birmingham, all blackened with smoke, the buses, the traffic, and the crowds of shoppers, proclaim this to be the centre of old Birmingham. As I drew, standing up among the jostling crowds, I realised that the left-hand side of the composition was going to be weak. The solution was forthcoming when a large double decker bus dashed down the road, leading the eye into the centre and providing an interesting piece of perspective. Likewise, the camber of the road caused it to lean a little, which seemed to add a touch of drama to this busy scene. Buses followed in quick succession, and never before had they received so much attention from me!

LICHFIELD, STAFFORDSHIRE

The Midlands are much maligned. Staffordshire has not kept a reputation for beauty — but here at Lichfield in a completely rural setting (only 16 miles from the centre of Birmingham) lies one of the most beautiful cathedral cities you can imagine.

The picture on page 144 shows the approach to the West Front, with seemly red brick houses on the left, and a long stone collegiate-type building on the right which form an exciting visual approach to the delectable West Front.

The Cathedral has had a history of endless destruction and rebuilding, but here it still is. That such a scene of serenity exists here in England is a matter for deep thankfulness.

145

THE RIVER KENNET AT MILDENHALL IN WILTSHIRE
This drawing could represent Southern England in one of its classic forms. The red-brick manor-farm, built perhaps in the days of Queen Anne. The village church much older, showing its bell-tower above the cottage roofs, the river with its gentle murmuration, slow-moving among the water-meadows — there are a hundred such scenes and all worthy of a picture.

The church, which has all its old pews and pulpit remains unspoilt.

WARWICK CASTLE AND THE RIVER AVON, page 146
This is another of the great classic views of England, which is beautiful at all times of the year. As a subject, the Castle has a tendency to become partially covered as the trees on either side of the bridge (upon which you are standing) grow wider. In this case, I went to the left end of the bridge to draw as much as I could of the right-hand part of the castle and then to the other end to do the same with the left part of the view. The arch in the centre of the river was once part of a mill and the little houses on the right are in Mill Street.

WALLINGFORD

This was drawn on three Market days in January a few years ago. I had long admired the place, particularly the happy juxtaposition of the Church and the Town Hall a most successful marriage of Mediæval and Palladian architecture. The buildings are at right angles to each other and so also are the sides of the Market-Square. This gives a strong feeling of serenity. Market days however, bring bustle and colour, and a lot of human activity, which I enjoy dealing with while trying not to block up the scene too much. The eye must always be able to find a way out of a picture, hence the roadway is allowed to come in at the right hand bottom and disappear away to the left centre, with an added exit on the right.

On my first visit the foreground was occupied by a fishmonger's stall. On my second and third the space was empty save for a pole with a notice fixed, on which was scrawled 'Closed until the end of January — gone fishing!'

WARWICK, LEYCESTER HOSPITAL, page 148

This large, half-timbered building adjoins the Western Gateway of Warwick. The upper part is the Chapel of the Hospital and a very fine group the two buildings make. But when I drew this picture I became dimly aware that there was something missing, and then I realised — some of the chimney-stacks, most beautiful and glorious things, had been taken down!

It proved to be true. I called and spoke to the Warden. He said 'Yes, they gave endless trouble, so we installed central heating and got rid of them. Now we can hardly afford the oil . . . so perhaps the stacks will all be put back'.

ABINGDON MARKET
I had often thought I would like to draw all the Townhalls, Guildhalls, Butter Markets, Market Halls, and the like which give charm to our market places, and bring them all into a book. They vary so much in design and material but all give pleasure to the eye. The finest is at Abingdon sketched here on market day.

OXFORD, THE COLLEGE BOAT CLUB BARGES, page 150
When this drawing was made for *The Illustrated London News* in 1956, already they were under threat from a variety of causes, but chiefly because of expense. A few were sold off to interested parties, but their future was bleak. Vast sums of money have had to be spent on maintaining the hulls to keep them water-tight and so the giving of parties to watch the races and the bumps on such attractive sites has come to an end. Oxford and the Isis are the poorer for it. A number of more efficient boat-houses have replaced the barges.

BLENHEIM PALACE: WOODSTOCK

One of Britain's few veritable palaces (for no other word can describe it) stands a short distance from the town of Woodstock in Oxfordshire. The area was a royal forest from before Domesday and remained so until the time of James II. Twenty-five years later, it and the New Palace, lately designed by Sir John Vanbrugh, was handed over by a grateful nation to John Churchill the first Duke of Marlborough, as a token of thanks for his victories, particularly at Blenheim.

HIGH STREET, OXFORD, page 152

'The High' is, just what a street should be. Full of varied and handsome buildings, it curves gently and widens, in the centre, giving a slightly enclosed feeling, but not too much so. It looks its finest at this very point in the middle of the road between University and Queen's Colleges, and where the buses stop. But it was only a few years ago that it became possible to stand and draw here for the road every day, from morning to night, was absolutely filled with slow-moving cars and lorries, until the by-passes were built (after much delay) and the authorities very kindly put down a narrow pavement in the *middle of the road* with a series of bollards, apparently expressly for me to rest my drawing board on! The tree on the right is surely the most felicitously placed of any. It manages perfectly to soften that stern, austere look one often feels in Oxford — in Cambridge never.

MARLOW, the church, river and weir from the lock
I never consider a summer has been properly used if I have not been up the Thames
Valley to paint a picture, Windsor, Maidenhead, Bisham, Henley Sonning . . . This is
Marlow and a very fine place it is too. Subjects here are innumerable. I am looking
forward to drawing Abingdon fróm the river. I've not done this yet, but it is very fine.

OXFORD, CHRIST CHURCH QUADRANGLE, page 154
One of the most handsome in Oxford, from any point of view. Here is shown the College
Chapel, opposite, with its beautiful Norman tower and spire, which, before Cardinal
Wolsey's days, was the church of St Frideswide's. He demolished part of it for his new
College.

King Henry VIII turned it into a Cathedral, carving out a new diocese from the
enormous one of Lincoln. Wolsey's college was done away with on the downfall of that
ambitious prelate and Christ Church College took its place. To the right is Christ Church
Hall, the finest in Britain, according to some authorities, after that of Westminster.

Dennis Flanders.

BESSELSLEIGH CHURCH

This charming little edifice could hardly be more different from Christ Church Cathedral, considering that they are both built as places of Christian worship. Besselsleigh church is situated near the main road four or five miles from Oxford, on the way to Farringdon in a very rural setting by the entrance to the park of Bessel's Leigh Manor. The interior is totally unrestored and perfectly charming. So far as the drawing is concerned, it was high summer and all the trees wore their full summer glory including this splendid copper beech.

CHRIST CHURCH CATHEDRAL, OXFORD (also the College Chapel), page 156

Ever since I first paid a visit to the superb and celebrated City of Oxford, my eyes and fingers have itched to draw this glorious chancel roof with its pendants and intricate vaulting. So, when I received a commission to draw it, it was not long before I began. So complicated is its construction that I do not think I have attempted to draw anything more difficult. I was also depressed at the fact that it has so often been photographed and drawn and always from the same point of view. So I withdrew to the west end, and stood beneath the organ loft, when suddenly I knew what to do. Utilise the two rather dull red curtains hanging there as a frame — and what a difference that made! Having arranged the curtains suitably and decided to paint them in a much brighter colour, I felt I had made a fresh impression of the inside of this beautiful church.

THE SOUTH COAST
FROM CORNWALL TO
KENT

ST MICHAEL'S MOUNT FROM MARAZION

The Island is made up of a mixture of early monastic remains and later domestic work.
The jetty and pier are early 19th century work, and there are a number of cottages. At
high-tide, the Mount is cut off from the mainland, as is its counterpart across the sea in
Normandy.

    This drawing was made from the hillside above the village of Marazion, in early May
when the yellow leaves were opening out from the trees and all the hedges and bushes
were a blaze of gold.

EXETER CATHEDRAL, BOMB DAMAGE

This was the result of one of Hitler's wicked 'Baedeker' raids. In this case the explosion brought down two of the flying buttresses that held up the main south choir walls and roof and created a highly dangerous situation. Mr. Godfrey Allen, the surveyor to St Paul's and organiser of the St Paul's Watch (of which I was member at the time) was summoned immediately — and saved the Cathedral by tying the choir wall to the opposite wall with steel bars until more permanent repairs could be carried out.

On the right is the Bishop's Palace and on the left, the Chapter House.

TOKENBURY, PENSILVA, NEAR LISKEARD, CORNWALL

This was a delightful commission. *Tokenbury* is a beautiful and comfortable home converted from a mill. The high ground behind is the fringe of Bodmin Moor. On the far right, you can see the mists rising from the Lynher River (for the day was going to be hot after a frosty night in early October.)

The black faced ram is called Casanova which was most suitable!

THE LIGHTS OF TORQUAY, (MOONLIGHT)
Vane Hill from Waldon Hill. This drawing was done entirely with carbon pencil, standing up, under a street-lamp after supper — for three or four evenings. Whatever has been built in Torquay recently can hardly have spoilt it much as its situation is so beautiful. It reminds one of Nice and its vegetation includes palm trees and other exotics that seem to flourish here.

BUILDING THE NEW TAMAR BRIDGE, page 162
A splendid engineering subject. Brunel's railway bridge stands behind the towers of the new road bridge and one of the last steam locomotives (a Castle Class) is working the afternoon train from Plymouth to Penzance across the bridge. On the opposite shore stands the Cornish town of Saltash which is full of subjects to draw.

WELLS, CHAIN GATE

Wells seems almost unbelievable when first visited. That such an enormous collection of mediæval buildings should remain to us, is a matter for deep thankfulness.

There is no end to such pictures in Wells. The bridge is known as the Chain Gate and connects the Cathedral to a unique street of mediæval houses. Beyond is one of the two beautiful western towers of the Cathedral.

PENSFORD, SOMERSET

This handsome viaduct (notice the variation in the thickness of the piers) straddles the
valley of the Chew and gives a dramatic touch to this view of a typical Somerset
village. It lies on the road from Bristol to Wells.

WELLS CATHEDRAL – from Tor Hill

All one's impressions of the beauties of Wells Cathedral and its immediate surroundings are perfectly framed from this point of vantage: it is the top of a modest hill, well covered with trees and bushes but cleared here for our particular pleasure. One may dream that nothing had been built here since the Cathedral was finished. I certainly did. The picture was drawn for a friend who produced it as a card to be sold by the Friends of Wells Cathedral.

WELLS CATHEDRAL – from the north-east
This is the view from the Fountain Inn, where I resided for a few days, in order to make
a picture of the east end of this Cathedral. The magnificent cedar tree makes the
centre-piece to this study of the Cathedral, with its three handsome towers, the Lady
Chapel on the left and the Chain Gate on the right. The road, in the foreground, is the
way into the city from Bath.

GENERAL VIEW OF BATH FROM BEECHEN CLIFF
One of the country's most beautiful cities, once the stage of fashionable invalids and now a centre of music and tourism. As a resort visited by the great ones of the land who bowed to the edicts of social behaviour laid down by Beau Nash, Bath escaped the provincialism of so many English country towns, and as a result succeeded in being a leader of fashion in all its forms, not least in architecture. In this drawing you can pick out the Royal Crescent, the Circus, North and South Parade, Great Pulteney Street, and many another famous street, while the Abbey dominates all.

This drawing was made in 1961 and shows a steam-hauled train entering Bath Station on its way to Bristol; the railway line, with its bridge over the River Avon, helps to hold the picture together.

THE AVON GORGE AT CLIFTON, BRISTOL

This view is very well known, and has been drawn and painted many times, but this does not prevent me from drawing it myself! It is a beautiful, fascinating subject, very unusual for Britain. Every single ship, using the docks of Bristol, once one of the greatest ports in Europe, must pass through this gorge, and under the great suspension bridge, that was a world wonder at the time. It was young Isambard Kingdom Brunel who designed it in 1831.

Somerset is to the left, Gloucestershire to the right, with the terraces of Clifton piling up one above another. But now it is all in the county of Avon.

High Street, Bath – Dennis Flanders 1952.

HIGH STREET, BATH (in 1952)
While certainly not the best known street in Bath (Pulteney Street, the Circus, the Royal Crescent, are all more famous) the High Street helps to form the incomparable beauty of this lovely City of the West. The Perpendicular Abbey, with its dramatically weathered stone stands beside the Guildhall built in 1775. Behind it are the Roman Baths and the Pump Room is only a few yards away.

BRISTOL, ST MARY REDCLIFFE, page 171
A drawing made a few weeks after the bombing of Bristol. Fortunately the church was left more or less undamaged for St Mary Redcliffe is one of the most beautiful and magnificent churches in the Kingdom. The first Queen Elizabeth thought and said so!

The damaged house shown in the centre was the scene of the poet Chatterton's death.

Other details show the great railway horses, still used in those days for pulling drays. The shunting engine is a GWR *King*. How are the mighty fallen!

KING STREET, BRISTOL, page 171
Bristol's heyday came with the discovery of the Americas and its imports increased enormously. King Street, cobbled and lined with old warehouses, almshouses, an ancient and famous Inn, with the masts of ships in the background expresses the real maritime air of Bristol.

The Llandoger Tavern is supposed by many to be the Spy-glass Inn, kept by Long John Silver in Stevenson's *Treasure Island*.

This drawing was done for the *Sunday Times* as one of the series of *Famous Streets*, and one importer of wine who spoke to me said if I put the number of his car in and it was readable, when published, he'd give me a bottle of brandy. I did and he did! Curious things happen when one is out sketching!

Dennis Flanders King St, Bristol

WINCHESTER COLLEGE

Inner or Chamber Court with Chapel Tower beyond and the Hall to the right. The College is one of the greatest and oldest of England's Public Schools, founded in 1382 by William of Wykeham, Bishop of Winchester, particularly for the education of the poor after the disastrous loss of clergy in the Black Death.

Adjoining the Cathedral and its stately precincts on the edge of the old City, and with the many-armed river Itchen passing by and under the area, the college is a rare and lovely thing.

An odd experience happened to me there. I left my camp-stool in an arch one day and when I returned from a stroll, it had gone. I told the porter about it and he called the Head Prefect to hear from me what had happened. "I'll do what I can" said he. "I think you will find it there tomorrow morning". I did. I was most impressed.

WINCHESTER, A GARDEN OF DELIGHT, page 172

Hurrying down each day from the Railway Station at Winchester to do some work at St Cross, a mile or so along the Itchen valley, it was my pleasure to go through the Cathedral Close and there are several different ways. I thought I knew them all but one day, finding another alley between a car park and the prep-school, I came upon this perfectly charming sight through a gap in the wall, as it were. Far too pretty pretty, says I to myself, hurrying on to my site at St Cross. But it haunted me like the sight of a pretty girl, and I knew I would be back and make a drawing of it — and here it is!

SUTTON VENY, WILTSHIRE
A beautiful Palladian house built about the end of the 18th century. There is a certain
amount of doubt as to who the architect was — there are two other houses in the
neighbourhood that appear to bear the same stamp.

It has been the home all his life of Major John Walker and his family. It was a great
privilege to be asked to make some drawings of his beautiful mansion.

SALISBURY CATHEDRAL, page 174
If Salisbury Cathedral, with its spire the tallest in the Kingdom, is one of the glories of
Southern England, its setting is that of mellow seventeenth and eighteenth century
domesticity. Around the lawns and trees of the Close, are many of the handsomest town
houses of the period, Mompesson House, the North Canonry, the King's House and the
Choristers' School.

BRAMSHILL HOUSE. HAMPSHIRE, interior of the hall
For a good many years now, Bramshill has been the Police Staff College. It is a vast
Jacobean mansion of the type of Hatfield and Audley End, and stands in the centre of an
enormous park. It was built in 1605–12 by Lord Zouche.

I had a set of six pictures to make here, of which two were made into prints. This
one is of the Hall and a very fine subject I found it. The doorway is of a beautiful design,
but it is the stone-screen that is the real centre of interest, emblazoned with shields in
heraldic colours.

WELLINGTON COLLEGE, CROWTHORNE, BERKSHIRE, page 176
The commission was to portray the view from the Master's house. It embraces the whole
of the south side of this enormous edifice. When I first beheld it, it appeared to me like
some vast palace in Europe, certainly not like an English country house. The architect
was John Shaw and it was opened in 1859 by Queen Victoria. I feel Prince Albert must
have had a hand in its design for, after all, he very much admired the German method of
education. It was founded in honour of the victor of Waterloo, whose estate, Strathfield
Saye, is not far away. Two of the School's most prized possessions are the Cloak and
Sword Wellington wore at Waterloo.

The idea was that the school should be particularly for the sons of officers and it still
has strong military connections.

HERSTMONCEUX CASTLE. SUSSEX
All rose red brick, an exquisite colour. This is drawn from the public footpath.
Herstmonceux is now the Observatory, moved down from Greenwich for clearer
atmosphere. I stayed at an inn in a village nearby while making this drawing.

CHICHESTER CATHEDRAL FROM THE BISHOP'S GARDEN, page 178
This is one of those scenes that only come to those who wait! Staying once with some
friends, in the Close at Chichester, in mid-summer, I was told the door into the Bishop's
Garden was unlocked one day in the week. I crept in and tip-toed round this place of
beauty and quietness. But it was the low sun that was throwing shadows across the lawn
and up to the Palace walls that *made* the scene. So I had to work quickly.

SHERBORNE CASTLE, DORSET

This work dates from February 1938, when I had the good fortune to visit the glorious town of Sherborne, in the company of the late Hanslip Fletcher, whose pen and ink drawings graced the pages of *The Sunday Times* for many years between the wars and after. He was making a picture of the famous school, but we walked up to the Castle in its park, just outside the town and liked it so much that we called! Colonel Wingfield Digby asked us to tea and gave me permission to draw. I made several quick sketches, the painting shown here being the only finished work.

This lovely honey-coloured house, built in the form of an H was begun by Sir Walter Raleigh in 1598 and finished some years later by the first Earl of Bristol, whose name was Digby. In 1684 William of Orange called here on his way to London having landed at Brixham, and printed his Proclamation to the people of London on a printing press set up on the hearth in the Green Drawing Room.

It has been the home of the Digby family since 1617.

Two vivid memories remain to me of this visit. The servants wore livery, and Mrs Wingfield Digby walked about the house surrounded by a cloud of Keeshonds (Dutch Chows), which she bred.

DISTANT VIEW OF CHRISTCHURCH, (page 180), The meeting of the Stour and the Avon. Early March.

See how the birds fly down to catch fish and echo the shape of the bent trunks of the old willow trees! Mother duck takes her brood for a swim. All around are rivers and waterways, with channels to the sea; anchorages, slip-ways, boat-building yards and the sea just across the bar. This is the atmosphere of Christchurch, which you must never call an appendage of Bournemouth, although it almost is. In Dorset now, it was a part of Hampshire until October 1974.

BODIAM CASTLE, SUSSEX

It is an empty shell, but a very fine one, and stands in the middle of a wide moat. Here again, the obvious view has appeared in a million photographs so I turned my attention to the oak trees which are a very rewarding subject for study.

RYE, SUSSEX, THE LANDGATE

As in so many drawings, it is the perspective and the poise of the central theme, the
Gateway, that makes the scene so interesting. See how the leaning cyclist helps the feel of
the roadway as it climbs and curves up to the arch.

AYLESFORD

Another example of a favourite genre of mine — a river, a bridge and a pile-up of houses, topped by a church, and surrounded by trees. This is Aylesford and the river is the Medway, the only real river in Kent! I've known it most of my life for it is very easy to reach by train from London, or you can walk along the river bank from Maidstone, a four mile stroll. Nearby, the old priory of the Carmelites has been restored and rebuilt; one of the most successful modern buildings I've seen. However, tragedy has struck. All the trees by the church were felled a few years ago — Elm disease.

BAKER'S CROSS HOUSE, CRANBROOK, KENT, page 185

Baker's Cross House stands guarding the eastern approach to Cranbrook, the capital of the Weald of Kent. It has a grand aspect set off by the elegant pillared porch in the centre. The history of the house has many twists and turns, and, as a result, it has been added to and altered many times. Built originally about 1740 the central part of the house including the porch retains its Georgian character. But the eye-catching mock-Tudor wing was added early this century, when the house belonged to Winch's Brewery. We have spent many holidays and weekends here as a family. It has a special place in our memories, a reminder of times past when summers seemed longer and hotter and winters were cosy and crisp!

MAIDSTONE from the Town Bridge, page 185

The most attractive scene in the busy and bustling capital of Kent.

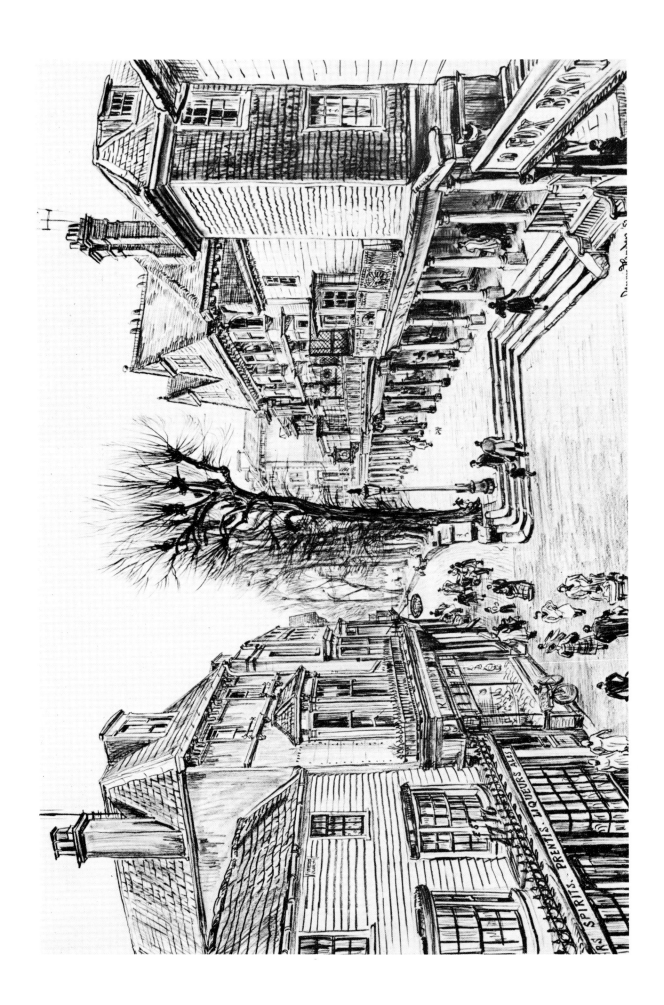

ROCHESTER
The Castle, the Cathedral, the Medway and a barge, all grouped together seen on a lovely afternoon in September. The creeper has grown along a part of the Castle wall and the balustrade in front was saved from the old Medway bridge, which the present one replaces.

TUNBRIDGE WELLS: THE PANTILES, page 186
In 1606 Lord North discovered the chalybeate spring that was to make Tunbridge Wells famous. Beau Nash and many other figures of the fashionable world of the 18th century strolled up and down this charming terrace of tile-hung houses which gave it its name. Most of the buildings with their arcaded shops were built after a fire in 1687. Antique and book shops, cafés of all kinds, seats, a bandstand, a pavement on two levels and a row of trees make this a quite exceptionally delightful spot.

APPROACH TO CRANBROOK
A typical row of Kentish houses on the right ending with an old house built round a
magnificent Tudor chimney. On the left is Rammell House, and its extension, a part of
Cranbrook School, which , like so many public schools is scattered over the village.

LEEDS CASTLE, KENT, page 188
The less said about this the better. It is too beautiful for words.
The only technical information I wish to mention is the fact that I have left out a
splendid beech tree that stands near the edge of the lake and appears to cut the Castle in
two. It is another case of not losing a perfectly beautiful and almost unbelievable picture
for a piece of unnecessary detail. Nelson also had a blind eye!

CANTERBURY CATHEDRAL AND THE DARK ENTRY

Words fail one when describing Canterbury. It seems incredible that so much remains, in spite of re-building and modernisation, not to mention the bomb that actually fell on the Cathedral Library (you see the rebuilt version between the trees and the Dark Entry). This drawing shows the north side of the Cathedral, from Green Court.

The gatehouse in the centre leads to the "Dark Entry", which title caused the famous author, The Rev. Richard Barham, to write a ghostly and murderous poem, in his *Ingoldsby Legends* to fit the name. There is certainly an air of mystery about this part of the precincts that may have suggested his tale. But when I drew the picture the sun shone, as it always does when I go to Canterbury.

EAST FARLEIGH AND THE MEDWAY, page 190

Here is the Kentish scene *par excellence!* The mediæval bridge, in steep perspective, the enormous willow tree in early autumn, the half-timbered manor and the distant oast-houses, all give character to this lovely composition. The great joy was drawing the wavelets and eddies in the water to show how the breeze affected the flow of the river as it passed by the cut-waters of the bridge.

THE CLOISTERS AT CANTERBURY
This was a private commission for a client very much concerned with the occasion shown.
The Queen has just distributed the Maundy Money to 39 poor men and 39 poor women
of the Diocese of Canterbury, and was being escorted back to the Deanery, through the
grey cloisters, this time enlivened with the crimson and gold of the Yeomen of the Guard.

CANTERBURY from the roof of the Odeon Cinema, page 192
Ave Mater Angliae is the title of this picture. It is the motto of the City of Canterbury and
one can hardly think of a better one. The roadway makes a perfect lead-in to the picture
and the two smoking chimneys give it a little extra life. The handsome weeping willow
tree has grown a great deal since I first drew the scene for the Fisher family who wished
to give the picture to their father, the late Archbishop, on his retirement.

LONDON AND ITS COUNTRYSIDE

WALTHAM ABBEY

I have known this all my life, in fact it was the first 'spot' my mother took me to sketch, for it is not very far away from where we lived, in Walthamstow. This actual drawing reproduced here, was made about thirty years later.

The scene is just on the edge of that hideous Lea Valley industrial area that is perhaps the ugliest approach to London. Waltham Abbey itself (and that is the name of the place as well as the church) is charming, with a little square called *Romeland* (like the one at St. Albans), and away to the east, the country rises up to the heights of Epping Forest. There is a farm nearby, and I have seen cows driven across the Abbey bridge and under the Gothic arch.

Inside the Abbey, itself, which is the Parish Church, the great Norman pillars are ornamented with deep spiral and zig-zag grooves, similar to those at Durham Cathedral. Peter de Wint, one of our greatest early water-colourists, came here and painted the same subject. He put in some chaps fishing from the bridge as their successors do today.

ST GEORGE'S CHAPEL, WINDSOR CASTLE

This is the Chapel of the Most Noble Order of the Garter, instituted by King Edward III in 1348, the highest order of Chivalry and whose Sovereign is the Queen.

The exquisite fan-tracery of the roof, worked out in pale-coloured stone is a fitting canopy to the gorgeous banners of the Knights and the wonderful dark-coloured screen, full of intricate and elegant carving. The stalls each have their shields and helmets and engraved plaques giving the coats of arms of previous Knights. This drawing took a fortnight to do.

ETON COLLEGE FROM ACROSS THE RIVER AT ROMNEY LOCK
This was done in January and mighty cold it was too. The Chapel is on the left. The poplar on the right has now gone.

RICHMOND BRIDGE, SURREY
One of the most elegant of Thames bridges, it must have been painted by more artists than any other bridge. Turner made a beautiful study of it, animated by lots of ladies in diaphanous dresses.

WINDSOR CASTLE
An irresistible subject, the enormous royal Castle, the red roofs of the town, the noble
trees, the slow-moving river, with its reflections and highlights. This is Windsor and the
piece of land on the left is a part of the playing fields of Eton, and the buildings, the Boat
Houses of the College.

WINDSOR CASTLE, THE HORSESHOE CLOISTER, page 199
This is a charming structure of timber and red brick set in an enormous area of stone. It
was built about 1500 for the Clergy serving the Royal Chapel of St George, (the steps
leading to which are seen in the right hand foreground.) The steep-gabled tower behind is
that of the Curfew Tower, the principal ornament of Thames Street down in the town.

HAMPTON COURT PALACE, THE ENTRANCE, page 199
This was drawn on a lovely summer afternoon and evening with the trees in full leaf and
lots of people enjoying themselves. Most of the buildings shown date from Tudor time.

GARRICK'S VILLA, HAMPTON, MIDDLESEX

A long time ago, a friend and I made a measured drawing of this jolly little Temple. He was training to be an architect, and I enjoyed the experience, for it was a lovely spot. Years afterwards (not so long ago, in fact), I went again to make a picture of it and was very annoyed to find that the tall beech tree which made such a handsome backcloth, had been drastically pruned. Also, some chicken-wire had been placed along the river-bank, either to stop children falling in, or swans and ducks from climbing up, or both. All this seemed entirely unnecessary so I left out the wire and went and drew another beech tree, (I forget where).

ISLEWORTH, page 200

Made during that summer drought of 1976, hence the lowness of the water. On the left is the famous public-house, *The London Apprentice*. To the right, the beautiful summer-house marks the western end of the Duke of Northumberland's enormous park of Syon House.

H.M.S. VICTORY, PORTSMOUTH

Possibly the most famous warship in history. What impressed me most was the thickness of the hemp cables. She is still a commissioned ship of the Royal Navy, and is visited by thousands every year. We place the drawing in this section of the book for comparison with *The Cutty Sark*, opposite. Both of them belonged to the high seas.

THE CUTTY SARK
The is the last survivor of the great fleet of tea-clippers that worked the China trade,
carrying cargoes of wool for much of the time. In 1890 she was sold to Portugal who ran
her until 1922 when she was bought back by a gentleman of Falmouth who restored her
in 1937. Ultimately after many vicissitudes and efforts by various people, she was
preserved and laid up in a new dry-dock at Greenwich, opened by H.M. the Queen to the
public in 1957.

THE HOUSES OF PARLIAMENT AND WESTMINSTER BRIDGE FROM COUNTY HALL

In my opinion this is one of the most exciting and beautiful views in London. I have drawn and painted this subject seven times — to date — and yet I still love it. Sir Charles Barry, the architect who won the competition for the design of the new Palace of Westminster was a classical architect so he employed A.W.N. Pugin to give expert assistance in designing the Tudor detail and so it is to the combined genius of these two great architects that we owe the romantic building which composes so well from every point of view.

ST PAUL'S FROM BANKSIDE

This is my latest version of the dearly loved scene — which seems to make a happy pair with the picture opposite. It is the view of St Paul's Cathedral from the Surrey shore, as seen at low-tide about 5 p.m. on summer evenings.

THE PALM HOUSE, KEW GARDENS WITH THE QUEEN'S BEASTS ON PARADE
In this wonderland of flowers, trees and plants, by the side of the Thames, stands this glittering pleasure dome of glass and iron, guarded by stone replicas of the Queen's Beasts, plaster originals of which were made by the Sculptor James Woodford for the Annexe to Westminster Abbey at Her Majesty's Coronation. The Palm House was built 1845–1847 to the design of Decimus Burton and Richard Turner.

ST BARTHOLOMEW'S HOSPITAL, SMITHFIELD.

The oldest hospital in London, dating from 1123 when Rahere founded a Priory here for the express purpose of healing. At the Dissolution the Priory was disbanded but the medical side was allowed to continue. In 1770 handsome new premises were designed by James Gibbs, the architect of St Martin-in-the-Fields, St Mary-le-Strand and the Senate House at Cambridge among other much-admired works. These buildings are very splendid and are still in use. Around them is an accumulation of later buildings, but trees, a fountain and lawns make an oasis of beauty in this rather arid part of London, which all help to bring patients, doctors and nurses alike to love the place. In area it is enormous and constitutes the whole Parish of St Bartholomew-the-Less. My picture shows the entrance gateway from Smithfield itself, put up in 1702 in memory of Henry VIII, whose effigy stands in a niche above the arch.

207

WESTMINSTER ABBEY, KING HENRY VII's CHAPEL
This is the crowning glory of Perpendicular Architecture and very difficult to draw!
It is the Chapel of the Most Noble Order of the Bath. The tomb, behind the altar is
that of Henry VII and his Queen, Elizabeth of York, by Torrigiano.

WESTMINSTER ABBEY, THE CHOIR LOOKING WESTWARD

THE RUINS OF THE COMMONS' CHAMBER

A drawing made soon after the bombing raid of May 10th 1941 which utterly destroyed the Commons' Chamber.

In the centre is the wall above the Speaker's Chair where was situated the Press Gallery, and the Ladies' Grille to whose mullions suffragettes chained themselves in 1908. What a piece of luck it was for me that the explosion left standing the amusing gargoyle on the right hand wall!

THE THEATRE ROYAL, DRURY LANE

This is another drawing originally made for *The Illustrated London News* in May 1963 to celebrate the tercentenary of the Theatre-Royal. This sketch shows the Ascot scene in *My Fair Lady*. It was done from a private box and took a week.

TRAFALGAR SQUARE
Some say this is the real centre of London. For many visitors it is. While traffic swirls around its perimeter, the broad, central part is traffic-free, a place for friends to meet, to talk and maybe feed the pigeons.

VIEW OF THE TOWER AND TOWER BRIDGE from the Headquarters of Toc H.
A drawing made for the Australian firm of John Sands Pty. Ltd., who have been fine
printers since 1837. They asked for a picture that was very much 'London' and this view
from a window near the top of the Headquarters of Toc H., seemed to me to be full of its
essence for in the Tower we have one of the oldest, and in the Tower Bridge, one of the
more recent, buildings in London. The White Tower was begun soon after the Norman
Conquest. There has always been a garrison quartered there, and you can see the
Barracks just to the left of the White Tower. In front of the trees you glimpse the Church
of St. Peter-ad-Vincula, the saddest spot on Earth according to Lord Macaulay, for the
bodies of those eminent personages executed on the block are buried nearby, some under
the flagstones of the church. The houses to the right include the quarters of the Resident
Governor of the Tower and the Yeoman Gaoler's house. Beyond the Tower Bridge (built
in 1894) you can see some of the wharves and cranes, now nearly all taken away.

ST STEPHEN, WALBROOK

As a picture this is the most dramatic of all those bombed church interiors I delighted in drawing. Delight was, of course, mixed with horror and terror that the damage might occur again at any moment. What could be done in the way of immediate restoration work was carried out as quickly as possible. I still have in my recollection, the horrid smell of wet and burning timber that hung upon the air for weeks around such sites. But what a lovely thing to draw!

THE TOWERS OF WESTMINSTER, marriage of H.R.H. Princess Elizabeth to Prince
Philip, November 1947
This picture came about as the result of a request from me to a friend whose office
window gave onto this superb vista. Yes, I was working on it for days before that of the
actual wedding, so that I could concentrate on the figures when the event was unfolding
itself.

The royal carriage is just leaving and the mounted police are saluting, while the
troops are presenting arms. I've never enjoyed a subject more. How frequently I had to
sharpen my pencils! In fact, I had several laid out on the window-sill already sharpened.

CHARING CROSS, LONDON
Every day, thousands of people arriving at Charing Cross Station see this scene — or do they? To me it has something splendidly Roman about it: each building, interesting in itself, is helped by its juxtaposition to its neighbours. I had seen it hundreds of times saying 'One day I will draw this, but what a lot of work!' A few years ago I began and it took literally, a month of Sundays, although I was greatly helped by a short railway strike when the station was closed and I was the sole occupant of the forecourt. From left to right — Nelson's Column, South Africa House with Charing Cross itself in front, The National Gallery, St Martin's-in-the-Fields and finally the 'pepper pots' of Nash's West Strand.

ST MARY-LE-STRAND, page 217 top
This and the neighbouring church, St Clement Danes, stand in the centre of the roadway and are a constant source of visual pleasure. St Mary's is my favourite London Church. The exterior from this point, shows the semi-circular apse, very baroque with all the mouldings throwing their long curved shadows in the morning as the sun moves round. Alas! much of this charm is now aborted by a frightful new building of King's College, London University, which was erected *too high* so that the church is shrouded in shadow save for a few hours only. Had the top two storeys stepped back a few yards further all would have been well.

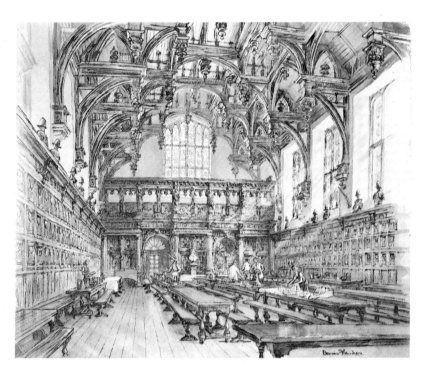

MIDDLE TEMPLE HALL
This is the only example in this book of a drawing featuring those marvellous timber roofs
of which there must be hundreds in Britain. They were used for churches as well as
houses and colleges, in fact, for any large chamber, and the one at Westminster is
considered, I believe, the finest. But this one at Middle Temple Hall, where lawyers eat
their lunches and dinners is certainly not far behind. The other, no less beautiful feature,
is the Jacobean Screen, with its wealth of richly-wrought carving. There is much heraldry
displayed in the stained-glass windows and on plaques fixed on the panelling — and
when the sun comes pouring in it is indeed a glorious place.

ST PAUL'S FROM NEW CHANGE

Every ten years of so, a violent desire comes over me to draw St Paul's again. Yes, I have drawn St Peter's in Rome many times, but, of the two, the Londoners' Dome is altogether finer, to my mind. It is utterly without that *ponderousness* that seems to emanate from St Peter's. Here, all is perfection of shape and proportion and the design is like that of the rarest sea-shell.

I made three studies of St Paul's this time. One from across the river, one from Cheapside, and this one from a new building occupied by the Bank of England, who kindly gave me hospitality and bought the original. It was the extraordinary spider-like scaffolding around the dome that caught my fancy and caused these three drawings to be made.

CORONATION DECORATION, WHITEHALL
Designed by Sir Hugh Casson and sculpted by Robin
and Christoper Ironside it was carried out in what
looked like silver and gold.

THE COAL EXCHANGE, BILLINGSGATE
Demolished in the mid-sixties, it is a very sad loss to
the architecture of London. It was designed by J.D.
Brunning, who was the architect of the Caledonian
Market and Holloway Prison. Besides bringing
delight to the eye, it was the perfect answer to the
visual problem of joining two streets which met at
right angles, but with a wide space in front.

ST PAUL'S CATHEDRAL, Moonlight and Blackout.
One fine and still night, soon after war was declared, the street lights are out and a few darkened lamps mark the kerb stones; the City Police wear their short cloaks and "tin hats" and the bases of the buildings are sand-bagged against the expected bombs. Everything is hushed, waiting for the war to begin in earnest.

   Six years later, when the All Clear sounded for the last time, St Paul's and the building on the left remained — the one on the right was destroyed. Since that time the Cathedral has been cleaned and the building on the left pulled down.

ST PAUL'S CATHEDRAL, page 220
When the renowned Noel Mander was appointed to rebuild the organ the first thing he thought of was how nice it would be to bring the two halves together on a screen as Wren had desired them to be and as they were until 1862, so he asked me to make this drawing.

BUCKINGHAM PALACE
This impression of the magnificent banquet given by Her Majesty to the French President and Madame de Gaulle, in the Ball Room on April 5th 1960, was commissioned by Sir Bruce Ingram and published as a double-spread in *The Illustrated London News* on 16th April of that year.

REMOVING THE ROOF OF CANNON STREET STATION, page 222
British Rail wished to demolish the roof of Cannon Street Station as the iron-work had to be painted every few years. But it was essential to keep the trains running. The engineers solved the problem most ingeniously. A heavy gantry was erected at the far end of the platforms. The whole roof was raised to run on ball bearings. When the cranes were set upon the gantry, the first girder of the roof was sawn into pieces and lowered onto trucks. Then the whole remaining roof was pulled forward by chains to the gantry and the second girder cut up and removed — and so on until all had gone. This operation took place in November 1958, and was a fascinating subject to draw.

VIEW FROM THE ROOF OF BUCKINGHAM PALACE

It seems suitable to end with the view from the roof of Buckingham Palace, done during the summer of 1949. It shows the London skyline, free of the modern high-rise buildings, with which we have now become so familiar. Big Ben is plain to see on the right and one's eye can pick out the Foreign Office, the lake in St. James' Park; the Dome of St Paul's; Nelson's Column and the Mall itself stretching away to the Admiralty Arch and on — on the left, the buildings of Carlton House Terrace and beyond, Piccadilly and Regent Street and all the area northward.

What struck me most forcibly was the country-house atmosphere. The Palace appeared to be surrounded by parkland, as indeed it is. To the North divided by the stately Mall are St James' Park and Green Park, while behind, is the garden, not very large, but the trees therein add to the countryside effect.

In the foreground, you can see the crowds that tend to gather there each morning to watch the Changing of the Guard, while the Memorial to Queen Victoria makes a splendid centre-piece to the circus.